Managers AS MENTORS

Building Partnerships for Learning

ALSO BY CHIP R. BELL

Customer Love: Attracting and Keeping Customers for Life

Beep Beep!: Competing in the Age of the Road Runner
with Oren Harari

Knock Your Socks Off Service Recovery
with Ron Zemke

Dance Lessons: Six Steps to Great Partnerships in Business and Life
with Heather Shea

Customers As Partners: Building Relationships That Last

Influencing: Marketing the Ideas that Matter

Managing Knock Your Socks Off Service
with Ron Zemke

Service Wisdom: Creating and Maintaining the Customer Service Edge
with Ron Zemke

The Trainer's Professional Development Handbook
with Ray Bard, Leslie Stephen, and Linda Webster

Understanding Training: Perspectives and Practices
with Fredric Margolis

Instructing for Results: Managing the Learning Process
with Fredric Margolis

Clients and Consultants
with Leonard Nadler

Managers AS MENTORS

Building Partnerships for Learning

SECOND EDITION, COMPLETELY REVISED AND EXPANDED

BERRETT-KOEHLER PUBLISHERS, INC.
San Francisco

Berrett-Koehler Publishers, Inc.
235 Montgomery Street, Suite 650
San Francisco, CA 94104-2916
Tel: (415) 288-0260   Fax: (415) 362-2512 www.bkconnection.com

Managers as Mentorssm is a service mark of Performance Research Associates, Inc.

Ordering Information
Quantity sales. Special discounts are available on quantity purchases by corporations, associations, and others.
 For details, contact the "Special Sales Department" at the Berrett-Koehler address above.
Individual sales. Berrett-Koehler publications are available through most bookstores. They can also be ordered direct from Berrett-Koehler: Tel: (800) 929-2929; Fax: (802) 864-7626; www.bkconnection.com
Orders for college textbook/course adoption use. Please contact Berrett-Koehler: Tel: (800) 929-2929; Fax: (802) 864-7626.
Orders by U.S. trade bookstores and wholesalers. Please contact Publishers Group West, 1700 Fourth Street, Berkeley, CA 94710. Tel: (510) 528-1444; Fax (510) 528-3444.

Printed in the United States of America
Printed on acid-free and recycled paper that is composed of 80% recovered fiber, including 30% post consumer waste).

Credits
Developmental editor: Leslie Stephen
Copyediting: Jeff Morris, Deborah Costenbader
Proofreading: Deborah Costenbader
Index: Randy Martin
Book production, cover design, and text design: Randy Martin

Library of Congress Cataloging-in-Publication Data
Bell, Chip R.
 Managers as Mentors: Building Partnerships for Learning/by Chip R. Bell - 2nd edition
  p. cm.
 Includes bibliographical references and index.
 ISBN 1-57675-142-2
 1. Mentoring in business. 2. Executives. 3. Employees—Training of. 4. Employees—Counseling of.
I. Title.
 HF5385.B45 1996
 658.3'124-dc20   96-7029

Second Edition
   06   05   04   03   02   01   10 9 8 7 6 5 4 3 2 1

CONTENTS

PREFACE

When I was in graduate school in the early seventies, one of my professors distributed a research paper entitled "Much Ado About Mentors." The thesis of this white paper was that four out of five Fortune 500 CEOs polled by the paper's researcher reported that their upward mobility to mahogany row was due in part to the positive influence of a mentor. When it came time for me to do a major paper in this course, I thought a paper on mentoring might be a favorite topic of my professor and net me an A in his course. One trip to the university library changed my mind. There was almost nothing written on mentoring in the world of work.

Some time later I took a position as the training director for a major bank. Wanting to be cutting edge with my 'wet behind the ears' eagerness and newly acquired graduate degree, I implemented a system-wide mentoring program for new professional recruits. The concept was simple — assign each trainee to a senior exec for monthly one-to-one 'show me the ropes' meetings along with formal classes on various aspects of general banking. The program was moderately successful, but, when the hint of impending recession came, it fell victim to the budget-cutting ax.

I remembered my professor's white paper and wondered why, if mentoring was so vital to success among the CEOs, it could not be salvaged at the bank, even in tough economic times. I managed to save face (after all, this was my baby) by convincing the chief budget sentry to let me continue a scaled-down mentoring program within one major division. My boss wisely added a conditional caveat: There was to be training for the senior exec mentors on how to mentor. That one addition saved the effort and the program was soon back on track for the entire organization. It helped me realize that mentoring prowess was not innate in those who held the rank of 'boss.' And I made a promise to myself to someday provide at least one book on mentoring to the university library I had searched in the seventies. This is that book.

There are people who are great mentors without ever having read a book or attended a class on mentoring. And there are a few rare souls who could read all the books and attend all the classes available and still come up short as mentors. This book was not written for either of these groups. Instead it was crafted for people who are eager to improve their mentoring aptitude. While mentors are the principal audience, it can also help protégés better understand the mentoring relationship. I will have more to say about this point later in the book.

Managers As Mentors, Revisited

I am a big fan of new. I rarely go to the same restaurant twice, even if it was a great experience. The ice cream shop nearby knows I will be the first on the block to try even the weirdest flavor of the month. The concept of a time-share — returning each summer to the same condo — leaves me absolutely cold. Why, I won't even eat leftovers unless my only other option is to skip a meal!

This is the second edition of this book. You would think I would abhor the idea of spending time on the 'leftover' version of a book. But I was enthused by the opportunity! This edition is not a warmed over version of yesterday's dish, served up with a different sauce on the side. I think you'll discover it has enough new and different ingredients not to be considered a leftover at all; rather, it is a completely new experience.

This new version is different in a number of ways. There are chapters in this edition not found in the first. There are also first edition chapters that I deleted. I learned a lot both from the feedback of readers of the first edition as well as participants in the mentoring workshops I conducted and keynote speeches I delivered. They helped me crystallize my thinking and enabled me to get a lot clearer on concepts that were somewhat vague in the first edition. I am grateful for the learning they provided me.

You will discover soon that *Managers As Mentors* is crafted around a mnemonic — SAGE — that forms the structure of the mentoring experience as I see it.

Surrendering (S) is all about actions that make mentoring a power-free experience. I have learned that power, authority, and command — or at least the protégé's perception of these traits in the mentor — can doom the mentoring experience to a perfunctory dialogue . . . sans risks, sans spirit, and sans discovery. The new chapter on trust making in this section provides a deeper exploration of the role and influence of authenticity (surrendering *to* the mentoring process rather than controlling it) in the quest for a power-free relationship.

Accepting (A) in the SAGE model focuses on the value of a safe, nontoxic relationship. When the protégé believes he or she is in a relationship that is not dangerous, growth-producing risk and experimentation are more likely to occur. The perception or prediction of danger is not related to physical harm, but rather the emotional damage caused by rebuke, judgment, or criticism — all of which yield a loss of protégé self-esteem in front of an important person. Why is this important? Without risk there is no learning; without experimentation there is no progress. The new chapter on acceptance makes the process of creating a safe climate and encouraging the protégé's courage to risk clearer and more pragmatic.

Gifting (G) is positioned as the main event in mentoring. Many mentors start their mentoring relationships with a gift of advice, feedback, or focus. However, when offered as the first step in the relationship, the act of bestowing such gifts risks their being at best undervalued, at worst ignored, resisted, or rejected. If Gifting follows Surrendering and Accepting, it is more likely to be experienced by the protégé as a sincere gesture and a valued contribution worthy of attention, try-out, and effort. There are five new chapters in this section. The gifts of advice and feedback had formerly been bundled into one chapter. Now they are split into two chapters and their new stand-alone status allows deeper, richer discussion. And new chapters on the gifts of focus, support, and storytelling have been added.

Extending (E) in the SAGE model formerly zeroed in on ways to extend the learning of the protégé beyond his or her relationship with the mentor. That is still an important goal. However, the central theme of Extending is now about the creation and nurturance of the protégé as a self-directed learner. In keeping with that theme, a new chapter on ensuring the transfer of learning has been added.

In addition, four new chapters entitled 'For the Protégé' have been included — one for each of the four stages of the SAGE model. Since the premise of this book is 'a partnership for learning,' the competence and comfort of the other half of the partnership is vital. Mentors may find these chapters helpful in seeing the process through the eyes of the protégé. In writing these chapters, I drew on the reports of protégés in order to see mentoring from their perspective.

The final two chapters explore two special but increasingly common mentoring situations. The first is 'off the beaten path' mentoring relationships — those involving peers, bosses, or protégés who are otherwise very 'different' from the mentor. The second special consideration is 'out of the ordinary' mentoring settings — by that I mean mentoring at a distance, in a hurry, or using artificial intelligence. Some of these topics appeared in the first edition. The new organization here plus new content is intended to help mentors manage these 'oddities' with greater productivity and success.

The new edition is not just a different book in its content and focus. What is also different are the times in which it is being released. Organizations scramble to attract and retain skilled employees. Mentoring can be a powerful weapon useful in winning the war for talent. And both the flattening of organizations and the transformation of the role of boss have left many managers in an identity crisis. Having risen up the hierarchy by virtue of their command and control skills, they enter a world where bossing is now about coaching and partnering. This book offers a new perspective on roles and competencies for bosses as an alternative to what it has meant historically to be in charge.

Organizations have always operated in a competitive arena. Whether vying for a share of an economic market, a share of the customer's loyalty, or a share of the resources doled out by some governing body, organizations operate in a contest mode. In today's race the winners are those that prove themselves more adaptive, more innovative, and more agile. These are the organizations populated by employees who are always learning, led by managers who are always teaching. So at a macro level, this book is about achieving organizational success.

When *Managers As Mentors* first came out, the concept of the 'learning organization' was new and popular. Peter Senge was the new management guru and his groundbreaking best-seller, *The Fifth Discipline*, was required reading for all contemporary, forward-thinking executives. We have today moved past the fad stage of a learning organization. The landscape of enterprise now is shaped by the dearth of talent, the pace of change, and the transformation of what it means to be in charge — all operating against the backdrop of a challenging economy. This new landscape has put 'helping employees grow' at the top of the list of critical success factors for all managers. Consequently, this book is more important today than it was when it first appeared in hardback in the fall of 1996.

As mentoring has grown in importance since then, so have the specifications for mentoring tools. Managers today want proficiency without having to buy into a program. They seek helpful resources and techniques, not hindering rules and policies. Explorations of philosophy and theory might be tolerated after hours, but in the middle of challenge and the heat of contest, managers shun any instruction not immediately transferable to their everyday practice. Consequently, this second edition has been written to be crisper, clearer, and — above all — more easily usable than the first.

How to Get the Most from This Book

Most books are written to be read from beginning to end. This is not one of them. However, you will benefit from initially reading the introduction and first section (chapters 1 through 3). Chapter 3 contains a self-scoring instrument referred to in several chapters throughout the book. To derive the greatest learning from those later chapters, complete and score this instrument first.

Before reading any chapter, start with a goal. Select a relationship you seek to improve, a skill you want to enhance, or a mentoring problem you want to solve. Choose the chapter that seems best suited to addressing that relationship, skill, or challenge. As you read the chapter, make notes on how you might apply the techniques you find. To help you zero in on the best chapter for your need, here is a brief description of the objective of each chapter.

Part I: Mentoring Is . . .

Chapter 1: The Art of Mentoring outlines what mentoring is (and is not), describes mentoring traps to avoid, and offers perspectives on how to make the mentoring relationship effective. This chapter also provides an overview of the mentoring model used to structure the book.

Chapter 2: Mentoring in Action: A CONTINUING CASE has a simple and singular purpose: to present the feel and drama of mentoring. Often participants in coaching and mentoring classes ask: Could you show a movie of what solid mentoring looks like, so we could know it when we see it? This chapter attempts to provide the screenplay for such a movie.

Chapter 3: Assessing Your Mentoring Talents: A SELF-CHECK SCALE is the chapter with the self-scoring instrument. Since several chapters have sidebars that apply the results of this instrument, I recommend that you read this chapter and do the self-check before going on to other chapters. Read chapters 1 through 3 first, then select whatever chapter fits your need.

Part II: Surrendering — Leveling the Learning Field

Chapter 4: Kindling Kinship: THE POWER OF RAPPORT makes the point that the way the mentoring relationship begins can strongly influence how effective it will be later. This chapter provides both perspectives and techniques for getting the mentoring relationship off to a solid start.

Chapter 5: The Elements of Trust Making: "THIS COULD BE THE START OF SOMETHING BIG!" shows how the quality of the mentoring relationship hangs on the success the mentor has in nurturing, communicating, and engendering trust. Using the style of the great comedian Steve Allen as the prototype, the chapter outlines practices important to trust building.

Chapter 6: Putting the 'us' Back in Trust: BLENDING HUMILITY WITH CONFIDENCE focuses on ways to narrow the emotional distance between mentor and protégé. This chapter outlines power-reducing techniques to create a level playing field for a mentoring relationship to be productive.

Chapter 7: Scared Students: WHEN FEAR AND LEARNING COLLIDE. One of the greatest barriers to learning is fear. Most leader-follower relationships have some element of anxiety, given the ever-present existence of position power (in the case of a boss) or expertise (in the case of a peer) or both. Likewise, most organizations still spend a lot of energy on evaluation, testing, and judging — all potential anxiety producers. This chapter examines ways to make a mentoring relationship a safe haven from apprehension for the protégé, thus a healthy environment for learning.

Chapter 8: For the Protégé: CALMING THE ANXIOUS HEART contains no secret 'for protégés eyes only' advice. It is the first of four chapters that underscore the premise that mentoring is a partnership. The better prepared both partners are for their function, the more successful the relationship will be. This chapter and the others like it take the point of view of the protégé as an invitation to both protégé and mentor to expand their view of their relationship. These chapters are placed as the last word on each stage of the mentoring process.

Part III: Accepting — Creating a Safe Haven for Risk Taking

Chapter 9: Invitations to Risk: ACCEPTANCE AS A NURTURER OF COURAGE. The process of moving from novice to mastery is clear. The protégé must embrace the risk of making errors and even ending in failure. To take such a risk, particularly in the presence of another, requires courage. And it is thus a key task of a mentor to communicate the kind of acceptance that will create a safe environment in which the protégé can experiment.

Chapter 10: Socrates' Greatest Secret: AWESOME QUERIES focuses on the power of asking questions to foster a protégé's feeling of acceptance. Everyone knows how to ask questions, but good mentoring uses inquiry as a tool to enrich the relationship while facilitating insight and discovery. Mastering the techniques in this chapter can benefit all interpersonal relationships.

Chapter 11: The Ear of an Ally: THE LOST ART OF LISTENING focuses on the importance and power of cultivating acceptance through listening. The initial temptation may be to skip this chapter, saying to yourself, 'I know how to listen!' Try to resist. Readers of the first edition indicated this chapter may be the most powerful one in the book because it offers a much deeper and richer definition of listening than generally discussed in how-to communication books.

Chapter 12: 'Give-and-Take' Starts with 'Give': DISTINGUISHED DIALOGUES is not a chapter about questions and answers. Rather it offers interpersonal tools on how to make a discussion more of an insightful (full of insight) conversation. This chapter takes Socrates' secret (chapter 10) to an advanced level of application, complete with techniques for restarting a stalled or sidetracked discussion or stopping a discussion that has become unproductive.

Chapter 13: For the Protégé: GETTING YOUR FEET WET WITHOUT WORRYING ABOUT DROWNING picks up where we left off in chapter 8. The continuing saga of mentoring from the protégé's point of view works through the acceptance stage of the mentoring relationship.

Part IV: Gifting — The Main Event

Chapter 14: Avoiding Thin Ice: THE GIFT OF ADVICE. Most people think the main thing mentors do is give advice — but if done inappropriately, advice giving is one of the most dangerous actions a mentor can take. This chapter provides techniques for giving advice while minimizing resistance.

Chapter 15: Reporting on Blind Spots: THE GIFT OF FEEDBACK. While advice is tricky to deliver without prompting protégé resistance, giving feedback is even more difficult. The by-product of advice poorly given is resistance, the reluctance of the protégé to value the information. However, the by-product of feedback inadequately delivered is resentment, a sense of bitterness on the part of the protégé that the mentor has a perspective unattainable by the protégé. Chapter 15 focuses on ways to make your comments count.

Chapter 16: Linking Proficiency to Purpose: THE GIFT OF FOCUS makes the point that adult learning must have a sense of rationale if it is to ensure the protégé's motivation and interest. This chapter outlines several approaches to anchoring learning in a fashion that guarantees relevance and purpose.

Chapter 17: The Bluebirds' Secret: THE GIFT OF BALANCE explores the role of balance in fostering growth. One of a mentor's most challenging dilemmas is to find a balance between providing guidance and giving the protégé freedom. The "when to hold 'em, when to fold 'em" challenge is especially tricky when the protégé approaches competence and independence.

Chapter 18: Once Upon a Time: THE GIFT OF STORY acknowledges the power of storytelling as a teaching tool. Most people count a parent, grandparent, aunt, uncle, or elementary school teacher as their earliest mentoring relationship. Lessons learned at an elder's knee were often laced with a 'Let me tell you about the time I . . .' instructive tale. Whether labeled parable, anecdote, fable, or yarn, stories can foster insight and discovery like no other tool.

Chapter 19: Passionate Connections: THE MENTOR'S GREATEST GIFT addresses the power of passion, spirit, and enthusiasm in the mentoring relationship. Countless studies have shown that the quality and quantity of learning are dramatically enhanced by the learner's excitement for learning. The mentor can play a crucial role in fostering this passion by displaying a sincere enthusiasm for the process.

Chapter 20: For the Protégé: ACCEPTING GIFTS WITHOUT GUILT. Being the protégé when 'gifts' are given can be awkward — similar to the way you feel during holiday gift giving when you receive a present and are not in a position to reciprocate. This chapter focuses on how to manage the awkwardness of this phase of the partnership.

Part V: Extending — Nurturing a Self-Directed Learner

Chapter 21: Beyond the Relationship: ENSURING THE TRANSFER OF LEARNING. The mentor's responsibility for the partnership does not end at the outer edge of the relationship. Successful mentors must look to ensure that what is learned makes a difference. This means remaining ever vigilant for barriers and obstacles that diminish the efficient transfer of learning.

Chapter 22: Managing Sweet Sorrow: LIFE AFTER MENTORING. Almost every mentoring relationship eventually comes to an end. The protégé outgrows the wisdom of the mentor; the protégé's learning needs shift to an area requiring a different mentor; the protégé or the mentor moves to a new role or place. How the relationship ends affects the readiness of both to establish new mentoring relationships. The parting is a potent platform for continuing growth.

Chapter 23: The Kaizen of Mentoring: LEARNING, LEARNING, LEARNING provides perspectives and resources for the mentor's continuing learning. Because effective mentors are more fellow learners than teachers, perpetual growth must be modeled and managed. This chapter shows how.

Chapter 24: For the Protégé: GROWING UP MEANS STEPPING OUT. The challenge of letting go can be acute for the mentor. It can also be prickly for the protégé who is suddenly being 'nudged out of the nest.' This chapter is a glimpse into how to get past the potential scariness of being a self-directed, independent learner.

Part VI: Special Conditions

Chapter 25: Unholy Alliances: MENTORING IN PRECARIOUS RELATIONSHIPS. Most of this book is concerned with traditional mentoring relationships. This chapter is examines some unique ones. Starting with mentoring situations in which mentor and protégé are equal — that is, peers — the chapter offers insight to situations in which mentor and protégé are enough 'different' to potentially impact how the relationship is managed.

Chapter 26: Arduous Alliances: MENTORING IN PRECARIOUS SITUATIONS. As relationships can be precarious, so can situations. This chapter looks at three unique complexities: mentoring in today's 'Time's up!' fast-paced work world, mentoring when protégé and mentor work in different places or have only intermittent contact, and mentoring with the assistance of artificial intelligence devices. Artificial intelligence devices are near-human voice recognition computers that can perform elementary coaching and even basic counseling. Albeit in limited use today, they are expected to play a considerable future role in tutoring employees.

Communicating Partnership

Words like 'mentor' and 'coach' are sometimes used to mean the same thing. Here is my distinction. Coaching is a part of the leadership role specifically aimed at nurturing and sustaining performance. Mentoring is that part of the leadership role that has learning (competence, proficiency, skill, know-how, wisdom) as its primary outcome. Granted, learning impacts performance, and that in turn impacts the accomplishment of important goals. You will encounter this definition more than once.

The words I use for the players in the mentoring partnership are chosen more for convenience than for any other reason. 'Mentors' are leaders who engage in deliberate actions aimed at promoting learning; 'leader,' 'manager,' or 'coach' would serve as well. Mentors do not have to be in a superior power position. One might easily be mentored by someone who is several levels below in the pecking order who possesses the needed skill or competence.

Some organizations find the label 'mentor' to have special negative baggage, often the result of ill-fated mentoring programs. 'Learning coach' is often a solid substitute. Likewise, 'protégé' refers to the primary beneficiary of the mentoring effort; 'associate,' 'subordinate,' 'colleague,' 'mentee,' 'partner,' or 'follower' could be used. As long as we are clear on who we mean, the labels can be changed to fit individual preferences and situations.

The main thing to remember is that this book is grounded in a partnership philosophy. It has no secrets aimed at making you look good to an unknowing subordinate, and I hope you will share it with your colleagues and associates and protégés. The more you know about how to mentor, the better the mentoring relationship will work for you. The same is true for the protégé. Some have found discussing the book helpful in improving the process of mentoring. Do what works for you.

As symbolized by the green trees on the book's dust jacket, both the mentoring process and the mentoring outcome are an unfolding, changing effort, like trees growing tall and healthy. The color green was chosen for its many connotations. Green has always characterized growth (the color of spring) and newness. Green traffic lights imply progress — they say, 'Go!'

Green can also connote prosperity. I hope you prosper from and enjoy this book. I would very much like your feedback on its usefulness, as well as your ideas on ways it might be improved in future editions. You will find my address at the bottom of the last page. Drop me a line, fax, or e-mail note, or give me a call. Happy mentoring!

Chip R. Bell
Dallas, Texas
September 2001

BEGINNING OUR JOURNEY

The vision for this book started in the seventies. But the impetus to put words on a page came from a retirement banquet a few years ago. I was a guest and the large northeastern company was my client. There was the usual band, banner, banter, and baked potato. There was also the customary nostalgia overload. Every aspect of the ceremony was well-trodden ground — until the final retiree was announced. For this person the applause was longer, the smiles broader, and the spirits higher.

The object of the crowd's affection was a forty-years-on-board security officer. The company president asked the security officer to come up onto the massive, over-decorated stage. The audience was hushed as he listed the security officer's accomplishments. The president was followed by several senior executives, each of whom praised the security officer as mentor and friend.

The president then announced a special gift for this mentor of mentors. Everyone waited in suspense. What special present could appropriately celebrate the contribution this man had made to so many?

The first clue was the stir and side conversations emerging from the back of the room as a man appeared in the doorway. I could hardly believe my eyes! Down the long aisle from the back door to the podium walked one of the most famous people in the business world. His tanned face was familiar to everyone in the room — and, for that matter, almost everyone in the country.

The surprise visitor walked straight to the security officer and embraced him warmly. With tears welling up in his eyes, he thanked the retiree for being a wonderful tutor during his two-year stint with the organization early in his career. After a few short stories about their association, he left the banquet hall to board his limo and fly in his private jet back to the opposite coast. The crowd sat stunned — no one spoke for a long time. Then, one by one, they filed to the front to express their gratitude to all the retirees.

I will never forget the power of that evening. It started me thinking about the gift of mentoring. What exactly had the security officer done to evoke such devotion? What contribution had he made to gain such universal admiration? The evening made me remember the many mentors who have blessed my life. It also prompted me to write down on paper what I had learned about mentoring.

The Power of Mentoring, Particularly Today

We inhabit a peculiar era in the world of enterprise. Revolutionary change renders skills and knowledge obsolete almost overnight. Peter Vaill's term 'permanent white water' has been used to characterize the feel of the workplace today. Likewise, success comes through creative adaptation and innovative break-throughs rather than from replicating the tried (tired) and true (not new). 'If it ain't broke, don't fix it' has been replaced by a new adage: 'If it ain't broke, break it.' Almost overnight, employees can go from champ to chump unless they stay perpetually honed and forever in a ready position. High-level knowledge require-ments are moving to low levels in the organization, meaning smartness can no longer be the badge only of bosses.

We are also living in a time when the war for talent is being waged ever more intensely. Young employees grew up with mobility the norm, not the 'one career, one company' mentality. Consequently, there is far less a 'jumping ship' stigma attached to frequent job changes. It makes talent reten-tion, especially in a brain-based economy, far more acute. A 2000 McKinsey & Co. study of seventy-seven companies and six thousand managers came to a similar conclusion: The most important corporate resource over the next twenty years will be talent: smart businesspeople who are technologically literate, globally astute, and operationally agile. And as the demand for talent goes up, the supply of it will be going down.

Customer requirements also bode for a different type of employee. No longer satisfied with a 'wowing' experience to ensure their loyalty, customers now want personalized, tailor-made products and services. To deliver such a 'one size fits one' offering, employees must be highly adaptable — able to learn quickly and respond flexibly. Customers recoil if they hear references to policy, 'our way,' 'we can't do it that way,' or any resistance around customization. And because cus-tomer acquisition costs are climbing and customers now drive an organization's economic performance, an organization can ill afford to sacrifice consumer ardor for corporate order.

All of this implies a requirement for a 'learning organization.' This term, made famous by Peter Senge in his best-selling book *The Fifth Discipline*, denotes an en-terprise that has growth, learning, improvement, and everlasting experimenta-tion woven into the fabric of its culture. "The ability to learn faster than your competition," said Arie De Geus of Royal Dutch/Shell, "may be the only sustain-able competitive advantage." Learning organizations value creativity over con-trol. They buck the tenets of old-style corporations by fostering an environment of risk taking. And in the war for talent, they are increasingly looking for new-style inducements for recruiting and retaining the best employees. Mentoring is now seen as one way to persuade employees to stay committed longer; the "Emerging Work Force Study," for example, reviewed in an early 1999 *Business Week* article, reported that 35 percent of employees who don't receive regular mentoring plan to look for another job within twelve months.

There is another factor of contemporary business life, now undergoing a major metamorphosis, that fuels the rationale for this book and the philosophy it represents: the relationship between boss and subordinate. The old model of leader as authority and corporate parent has been and continues to be altered to one of leader as supporter, enabler, even partner. As workers increasingly demonstrate that they have the maturity and competence to operate effectively with limited supervision, empowerment has become a necessity rather than a fad. Leaders unable to let go of the reins of power are fast being replaced by leaders who view their relationship with associates as being that of liberator, barrier remover, facilitator — and mentor.

The requirement for constant learning and the modification of the leader's role call for a new kind of manager. This book has been crafted to provide supervisors and managers both the competence and the confidence to address these two factors. Although managers frequently perform their bossing in a group context, as with a team, the lion's share of the manager's time is spent one on one. Therefore, this book largely focuses on the interpersonal encounters of leaders. Mentoring is predominately a one-person-at-a-time activity.

Managing As Mentoring

This book is titled 'Managers As Mentors.' But, in truth, it is really about 'managing as mentoring.' The philosophy of the effective mentor is the stuff great leaders are made of. Mentoring is about *Surrendering* (meaning surrendering to the process rather than controlling the process), *Accepting* (meaning using actions that create a safe haven for experimentation and risk taking), *Gifting* (meaning providing the gifts of advice, feedback, story, support, and focus), and *Extending* (meaning helping the protégé become a self-directed learner).

These building blocks are also the tools for effective leadership. Great leaders are confident enough to show *humility*. And humility promotes a partnering relationship rather than a parenting relationship. Great leaders create emotional safety through the *courage* and the attentive *curiosity* they foster IN others. Great leaders are generous with their *advice* (given in a fashion that does not surface resistance), their *feedback* (delivered in a manner that does not unearth resentment), their *stories* (told in a way that stirs passion as well as sparks insight), their *support* (provided to ensure their associates have backing and assistance), and their *focus* (given to ensure associates have a sense of direction, purpose, and vision). Now, look back on all the words in italics and you will discover the human architecture of today's leader. The way of the mentor is the way of the leader, particularly in today's brain-based economy.

The definition of leader could be expanded to include anyone in a role (short or long term) whose primary goal is to influence another to important efforts or outcome. Given the flattening of organizations, more often than not the mentoring a person receives may come from a peer. It is also not unusual for leaders to get mentoring from people below them in the organization. So, the leader in the learning arena is best described as the person with competencies she or he is willing to share. For all these reasons, I have included a chapter on 'unholy alliances' — those mentoring situations in which the positions or relationship of mentor and protégé fall outside the norm. Additionally, there is a chapter at the end of every section called 'For the Protégé.' My hope was that protégés would find this book a useful resource too. I encourage you to read it, especially if you are the mentor, to gain a peephole into the way protégés think and feel during a mentoring experience.

Mentoring as Problem Solving

We live in times when a subject's relevance is a function of its capacity to solve our everyday problems. *Managers As Mentors* is intended to be problem-solving tool. Some typical workplace problems are framed in the questions below. Do a bit of soul-searching as you consider your answers. I'll check back with you at the end.

- Are you concerned that your team, unit, or organization may be slipping in its ability to attract and retain the most talented people?

- Do your worry that your team, unit, or organization may be falling behind others in your peer group?

- Do you sense that too many people in your team, unit, or organization may be bored and just going through the motions too much of the time?

- Do customers of your team, unit, or organization complain that employees don't seem to know what they're doing or are not finding a tailored solution or response to a customer's need or request?

- Are managers resorting to an impatient 'telling' mode when a less directive approach would engender far greater motivation and more learning among employees?

- When you offer an employee advice do you get the feeling your advice never really registers?

- When you give an employee feedback, do you sense a bit of resentment or defensiveness?

- Have efforts you've made in the past to help an employee learn ever not actually translated into improved performance . . . as though it didn't really 'take?'

- Have you wondered why employees fail to come to you for guidance and instead simply go it alone to figure out their own role or performance?

- Are you not finding time to train because there's barely enough time to get the work done?

- Has someone suggested that you mentor your employees and you find yourself uncertain about to what that means and how to do it?

- Do you need to mentor someone very different from you and find yourself feeling anxious about what that implies?

- Have you been the victim of a company "mentoring program" that failed to realize most of the benefits on which it was sold?

- Are you loosing sleep at night worried about your future?

I'm back. This book is crafted to address all of the questions outlined above

— well, maybe not that last one! Your sleepless nights may not have anything to do with being mentor-challenged. But all of the other issues can be addressed and resolved with the concepts and techniques to follow. However, there's an important caution. All the mentoring wisdom in the world is only effective if it is tried, tried again, and continually practiced. The hike from greenhorn to greatness is fraught with stubbed toes, missteps, and a few skinned knees so to speak. Be patient with your new learning and give it a chance to become a part of how you lead by first becoming a part of who you are.

Mentoring as an Art

The mentor is a teacher, a guide, a sage, and foremost a person acting to the best of his or her ability, in a whole and compassionate way in plain view of the protégé. No greater helping or healing can occur than that induced by a model of compassion and authenticity. Mentoring is about being real, being a catalyst, and being sometimes a kind of prophet. It is therefore far more art than science. It is about personal power, not expert or role power. The most powerful and most difficult part of mentoring is being who you are.

This is not to imply that a mentor must be some kind of superhero without flaws, doubts, or the capacity for making mistakes. Fundamentally, mentoring is about growing — mentors with growing protégés, protégés growing with mentors. The core of a mentoring relationship is more about a mutual search than imparting wisdom. As a collective pursuit, mentoring works best when mentors are focused on building, not boasting.

The anthropologist Carlos Castaneda used the word 'magic' to describe his unique mentoring relationship with the Yaqui medicine man, Don Juan — and truly there is a magical quality to the mentoring process when it takes on a life of its own and leads mentor and protégé through an experience of shared discovery. The challenge of helping another see things in a new way has had many labels down through the centuries. Biblical writers used fishing analogies to capture the spirit of mentoring magic and told of removing scales from eyes. The philosopher Ram Dass referred to it as 'a dance.'

Mentoring magic cannot be a solo performance. It is not a one-way, master-to-novice transaction. To be effective and lasting, it must be accomplished through a two-way relationship — the synchronized efforts of two people. The synchrony and synergy of mentoring are what give it a dance-like quality. They are also what make it magical.

This is not the first book on mentoring — nor the last. But from what I have seen, it is the only one to date that is grounded in a true partnership philosophy. My take on mentoring with a partnership philosophy is this: Assume that all your future employees will be independently wealthy, headstrong, purpose-seeking volunteers who love to acquire learning but hate to surrender liberty.

This book is also about power-free facilitation of learning. It is about teaching through the power of consultation and collaboration rather than constriction and assessment. It views learning as an expansive, unfolding process rather than an evaluative, narrowing effort. It is a song about unfolding — one in which the last few stanzas have yet to be written. It is the instruction book on how to perform synchronized magic.

This is not a philosophy book, although it is grounded in very specific convictions: that the principal goal of mentoring is to create a self-directed learner, that the primary tool for learning is discovery, and that the most effective context for reaching that goal is a learning partnership. This is a workbook, filled with ideas, suggestions, how-tos, and resources. If it ends up dog-eared, underlined, and passed around, it will mean that I have succeeded in making it a practical book — perhaps even a fun book as well as a soul-searching one. It is intended to be a tool for a critical component of the leader's responsibility — helping another learn and grow.

Managers AS MENTORS

Building Partnerships for Learning

Part I

Mentoring Is . . .

Mentoring Is ...

Take a minute to recall the people in your life who were effective at helping you learn something important. (I'll wait.) My mother taught me a lot about dating etiquette when I was a teenager; my son, Bilijack, showed me some awesome soccer plays and my daughter-in-law, Lisa, showed me creative ways to make a party announcement. Over the course of our lives, learning comes from many people, in many places, and through many events.

What are the reasons that people sometimes learn and sometimes fail to learn? What are the reasons that some people are skilled at helping others with personal or professional growth and some are not? Why does mentoring sometimes make an impact and at other times seem a complete waste of time and energy? What conditions and competencies spark discovery, insight, and understanding?

The complete answers to questions like these could occupy volumes — and you're holding only a single book. As you will see, there *are* tools, tips, tactics, and techniques that make mentoring easier to understand, more effective, and a lot more fun — but to become good at the game, we must first mark off the playing field. Before we learn the pointers, we need to be clear on the meaning of mentoring and in harmony with the conditions conducive to its effectiveness.

> "Learning is not attained by chance, it must be sought for with ardor and attended to with diligence."
>
> — Abigail Adams (1780)

The goal of the next three chapters is to explain the arena or context of mentoring. Mentoring will be defined as 'the act of helping another learn.' Mentoring is traditionally thought of as a transaction between a tutor and somebody else's subordinate. However, *Managers As Mentors* will focus largely on the leader mentoring a follower. This will require a unique alteration in the relationship — actions aimed at eliminating (or at least reducing) the role that position power plays in the tutelage.

The mentoring arena is filled with assumptions about how people learn, roles mentors can play, qualities mentors should pursue, and traps mentors need to avoid. Since the mentor is also a learner, the intent of the next few chapters is to prompt self-examination, to advocate clarity of mission, and to nurture the linkage of who we are with what we do.

CHAPTER 1
The Art of Mentoring

Mentor: The word conjures up an image of a seasoned corporate sage conversing with a naïve, wet-behind-the-ears young recruit. The conversation would probably be laced with informal rules, closely guarded secrets, and 'I remember back in seventy-seven . . .' stories of daredevil heroics and too-close-to-call tactics. Mentoring has an almost heady, academic sound, reserved solely for workers in white collars whose fathers advised, 'Get to know ol' Charlie.'

More recently the term 'mentor' became connected less with privilege and more with affirmative action. Minority employees got assigned a mentor to expedite their route through glass ceilings, beyond old-boy networks and the private winks formerly reserved for WASP males. Such mentors sometimes salved the consciences of those who bravely talked goodness but became squeamish if expected to spearhead courageous acts. These mentoring programs sounded contemporary and forward thinking. Some were of great service, but many were just lip service.

But what is mentoring, really? When the package is unwrapped and the politically correct is scraped away, what's left? A mentor is defined in the dictionary as 'a wise, trusted advisor . . . a teacher or coach.' Such a simple definition communicates a plain-vanilla context. In case you missed the preface, mentoring is defined as that part of the leader's role that has learning as its primary outcome. Bottom line, a mentor is simply someone who helps someone else learn something that would have otherwise been learned less well, more slowly, or not at all. Notice the power-free nature of this definition; mentors are not power figures.

The traditional use of the word 'mentor' denotes a person outside one's usual chain of command — from the junior's point of view, someone who 'helps me understand the informal system and offers guidance on how to be successful in this crazy organization.' Not all mentors are supervisors, but most effective supervisors act as mentors. Mentoring is typically focused on one person; group mentoring is training or teaching. We will focus on the one-to-one relationship; the others are beyond the scope of this book.

Good leaders do a lot of things in the organizations they inhabit. Good leaders communicate a clear vision and articulate a precise direction. Good leaders provide performance feedback, inspire and encourage, and, when necessary, discipline. Good leaders also mentor. Once more, mentoring is that part of a leader's role that has growth as its primary outcome.

LESSONS FROM THE FIRST MENTOR

The word 'mentor' comes from *The Odyssey*, written by the Greek poet Homer. As Odysseus ('Ulysses' in the Latin translation) is preparing to go fight the Trojan War, he realizes he is leaving behind his one and only heir, Telemachus. Since 'Telie' (as he was probably known to his buddies) was only in junior high, and since wars tended to drag on for years (the Trojan War lasted ten), Odysseus recognizes Telie needs to be coached on how to 'king' while Daddy is off fighting. He hires a trusted family friend named Mentor to be Telie's tutor. Mentor is both wise and sensitive — two important ingredients of world-class mentoring.

The history of the word 'mentor' is instructive for several reasons. First, it underscores the legacy nature of mentoring. Like Odysseus, great leaders strive to leave behind a benefaction of added value. Second, Mentor (the old man) combined the wisdom of experience with the sensitivity of a fawn in his attempts to convey kinging skills to young Telemachus. We all know the challenge of conveying our hard-won wisdom to another without resistance. The successful mentor is able to circumvent resistance.

Homer characterizes Mentor as a family friend. The symbolism contained in this relationship is apropos to contemporary mentors. Effective mentors are like friends in that their goal is to create a safe context for growth. They are also like family in that their focus is to offer an unconditional, faithful acceptance of the protégé. Friends work to add and multiply, not subtract. Family members care, even in the face of mistakes and errors.

Superior mentors know how adults learn. Operating out of their intuition or on what they have learned from books, classes, or other mentors, the best mentors recognize that they are, first and foremost, facilitators and catalysts in a process of discovery and insight. They know that mentoring is not about smart comments, eloquent lectures, or clever quips. Mentors practice their skills with a combination of never-ending compassion, crystal-clear communication, and a sincere joy in the role of being a helper along a journey toward mastery.

Just like the first practitioner of their craft, mentors love learning, not teaching. They treasure sharing rather than showing off, giving rather than boasting. Great mentors are not only devoted fans of their protégé, they are loyal fans of the dream of what the protégé can become with their guidance.

TRAPS TO AVOID

There are countless traps along the path of mentordom. Mentoring can be a power trip for those seeking an admirer, a manifestation of greed for those who must have slaves. Mentoring can be a platform for proselytizing a cause or crusade, a strong tale told to an innocent or unknowing listener. However, the traps of power, greed, and crusading all pale when compared with the subtler 'watch out fors' listed below. There are other traps, of course, but these are the ones that most frequently raise their ugly heads to sabotage healthy relationships.

Keep the traps in mind as you read the rest of the book; search for them within yourself. By the time you've read the last page, you will perhaps have learned to avoid those to which you are most susceptible.

I Can Help

When is help helpful, and when is it harmful? People inclined to be charitable with their time, energy, and expertise often try to help when what the learner actually needs is to struggle and find her own way. Here's a test: If you ask the protégé, 'May I help?' and she says no, how do you feel? Be honest with yourself. If you react with even a trace of rejection and self-pity, this may be your trap to avoid.

I Know Best

Some people become mentors because they enjoy being recognized as someone in the know. They relish the affirmations from protégés who brag to others about their helpful mentor. They especially like protégés who regularly compliment them on their contribution. This is a trap! You may get off track and end up using the protégé for your own recognition needs. The test? If your protégé comes to you and says that he has found someone else who might be more helpful as a mentor, how do you react? If you feel more than mild and momentary disappointment, beware! This may be your special trap.

I Can Help You Get Ahead

Mentors can be useful in getting around organizational barriers, getting into offices otherwise closed, and getting special tips useful in climbing the ladder of success. As sometime king makers, their promises carry an 'I can get it for you wholesale' seduction. All these 'gettings' can be valuable and important. They can also add a bartering, sinister component to an otherwise promising relationship. The 'You scratch my back, and . . .' approach to mentoring relationships can infuse a score-keeping dimension that is detrimental to both parties. Although reciprocity can be important, a tit-for-tat aspect can lead one person in the relationship to a score-keeping, 'You owe me one' view of the relationship.

You Need Me

When mentors feel that their protégés need them, they are laying the groundwork for a relationship based on dependence. Although many mentor-protégé partnerships begin with some degree of dependence, the goal is to transform the relationship into one of strength and interdependence. A relationship based on dependence can ultimately become a source of resentment for the protégé, false power for the mentor.

If the protégé views the mentoring process as a chore or a necessary ritual, it is generally a dependent relationship that will not be allowed to grow up. Remember, the focus should be on helping the protégé become strong, not on helping the protégé feel better about being weak.

THE QUALITIES OF GREAT MENTORING

Great mentors are not immune to traps; great mentors recognize the traps they are likely to fall into and work hard to compensate for them. How do they do that? They do it by understanding the qualities of a mentor-protégé relationship focused on discovery and learner independence — and then learning to be living, breathing models of those qualities.

First and foremost, great mentoring is a partnership. And partnership starts with balance.

Balance

Unlike a relationship based on power and control, a learning partnership is a balanced alliance, grounded in mutual interests, interdependence, and respect. Power-seeking mentors tend to mentor with credentials and sovereignty;

partnership-driven mentors seek to mentor with authenticity and openness. In a balanced learning partnership, energy is given early in the relationship to role clarity and communication of expectations; there is a spirit of generosity and acceptance rather than a focus on rules and rights. Partners recognize their differences while respecting their common needs and objectives.

Truth

Countless books extol the benefits of clear and accurate communication. Partnership communication has one additional quality: It is clean, pure, characterized by the highest level of integrity and honesty. Truth-seekers work not only to ensure that their words are pure (the truth and nothing but the truth), but also to help others communicate with equal purity. When a mentor works hard to give feedback to a protégé in a way that is caringly frank and compassionately straightforward, it is in pursuit of clean communication. When a mentor implores the protégé for candid feedback, it is a plea for clean communication. The path of learning begins with the mentor's genuineness and candor.

Trust

Trust begins with experience; experience begins with a leap of faith. Perfect monologues, even with airtight proof and solid support documentation, do not foster a climate of experimentation and risk taking. They foster passive acceptance, not personal investment. If protégés see their mentors taking risks, they will follow suit. A 'trust-full' partnership is one in which error is accepted as a necessary step on the path from novice to master.

Abundance

Partnership-driven mentors exude generosity. There is a giver orientation that finds enchantment in sharing wisdom. As the 'Father of Adult Learning' Malcolm Knowles says, "Great trainers [and mentors] love learning and are happiest when they are around its occurrence." Such relationships are celebratory and affirming. As the mentor gives, the protégé reciprocates, and abundance begins to characterize the relationship.

Passion

Great mentoring partnerships are filled with passion; they are guided by mentors with deep feelings and a willingness to communicate those feelings. Passionate mentors recognize that effective learning has a vitality about it that is not logical, not rational, and not orderly. Such mentors get carried away with the spirit of the partnership and their feelings about the process of learning. Some may exude emotion quietly, but their cause-driven energy is clearly present. In a nutshell, mentors not only love the learning process, they love what the protégé can become — and they passionately demonstrate that devotion.

Courage

Mentoring takes courage; learning takes courage. Great mentors are allies of courage; they cultivate a partnership of courageousness. They take risks with learning, showing boldness in their efforts, and elicit courage in protégés by the examples they set. The preamble to learning is risk, the willingness to take a shaky step without the security of perfection. The preamble to risk is courage.

Partnerships are the expectancy of the best in our abilities, attitudes, and aspirations. In a learning partnership, the mentor is not only helping the protégé but also continually communicating a belief that he or she is a fan of the learner. Partnerships are far more than good synergy. Great partnerships go beyond 'greater than' to a realm of unforeseen worth. And worth in a mentoring partnership is laced with the equity of balance, the clarity of truth, the security of trust, the affirmation of abundance, the energy of passion, and the boldness of courage.

THE REAL AIM OF MENTORING: MASTERING, NOT MASTERY

My friend George has never been a person of moderation. When he and I were in college and a few of us took a forbidden midnight swim in the pool at the girl's gym on the other side of a locked fence, he was the one who decided we should make it a skinny dipping adventure. The fact that none of us stripped but George never seemed to bother him. It was not surprising to me that years later, after reading the best-selling book *Swim with the Sharks without Being Eaten Alive*, George went to a pet store and bought a live shark for his Miami apartment. Though just six inches long, it was a real shark — with a distinctive white dorsal fin rising out of his gun-metal gray body. George named the little fish Harvey after the book's author, Harvey Mackay.

Sometime later, George's life took an unexpected turn. He was promoted to regional sales manager of his company and transferred to Houston. Knowing he was going to be on the road a lot, George worried about who would take care of little Harvey. So he gave the shark to Sea World. Harvey moved from a two-gallon fish bowl to an aquarium the size of a three-story house.

Several years went by. When he got married, the inextinguishable kid in George picked Walt Disney World as the perfect honeymoon site. While he and his wife were in Orlando, they decided to go by Sea World and check on little Harvey. They were stunned. Harvey now was almost six feet long and weighed nearly one thousand pounds.

When George told me about Harvey, I thought it was another of his tall tales. But he convinced me it was true. Apparently certain animals — like sharks, and like humans — grow commensurate with their surroundings. If we are to grow to our greatest potential, we need a safe and unrestricted environment.

To grow is fundamentally the act of expanding, an unfolding into greatness. And so expansiveness is the most important attribute of a great mentoring relationship. Mentoring effectiveness is all about clearing an emotional path to make the learning journey as free of boundaries as possible. Change is a door opened from the inside. But it is the mentoring relationship that delivers the key to that door.

> "It is much easier to be critical than to be correct."
> — Benjamin Disraeli

The real aim of mentoring is not mastery. Mastery implies closure, an ending, arrival at a destination. In today's ever changing world, the goal is 'mastering,' a never-ending, ever expansive journey of perpetual growth. It suggests the relationship is more important than the goal, that the process is more valued than the outcome.

BUSTING THE BOUNDARIES

So, what can a mentor do to set up an expansive, boundary-free learning environment? Extensive research shows that great mentors give unswerving attention to four essential components: focus, feeling, family, and freedom.

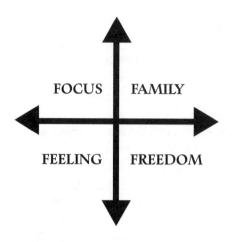

FIGURE 1. COMPONENTS OF EXPANSIVE LEARNING ENVIRONMENTS

Focus

There are several ways adult learning (andragogy) is different from child learning (pedagogy). Adults are motivated to learn when they perceive an immediate or short-term rationale for that learning. You can tell a child, 'This history you are learning in the classroom may not be useful on the playground at recess, but *someday* it will be helpful to you' and retain their interest. Adults are not so gullible. Granted, some adults get a kick out of learning purely for learning's sake. But they are in the minority. Most adults are motivated to learn if the effort will have a clear payoff in the present or — at most — in the very near future.

The mentoring partnership must be conducted so that the protégé knows the purpose of the learning. There needs to be an 'as a result of this learning, you will be able to . . .' component woven through your partnership. In the organizational context, it helps to anchor the learning to the unit or organizational vision or mission, to unit objectives, and to the protégé's personal or professional goals and aspirations. The tie must be subtle . . . and at the same time obvious. It should be an initial focus . . . and a perpetual one. Anchoring learning to objectives is one way to create useful guideposts for measuring success. Think of focus as not only the basis for your interaction, think of it as the very language you speak.

Feeling

Do you remember what you learned about relationships when you were in high school? Remember that friendship that went sour and how you worked so hard to get it back together? Remember going steady, breaking up, having fights, making up . . . and on and on? The lessons learned in those heart-pain days seem indelibly etched in our memories. They are the lessons we teach our children, nieces or nephews, or friends' children.

Now think about other things you learned in high school. Maybe you learned sine, cosine, and tangent. You learned to conjugate verbs and diagram sentences. You knew the length of the Amazon River and the height of the Empire State Building or the Eiffel Tower. You could name the capital of every state in the union. And you probably got A's on those tests. Remember? If there were a pop quiz today, how would you fare? Somehow, learning that is not anchored to the heart is not retained.

The mentoring relationship is at its best when it is conducted with spirit and emotion. I had the honor (some would say dishonor) of serving in the late sixties in Vietnam as an infantry unit commander. Before going into combat I spent almost a year in officer training. I can remember intricate details of most of my tour in combat and only vaguely the time spent in training. The lessons learned in combat were lessons of the heart, imprinted with the passion of the most exhilarating highs and the most depressing lows. Part of the mentor's job is to foster an environment where feelings, emotions, and learning are tightly linked.

Family

Mentoring works best when implemented in the spirit of partnership. In *The Fifth Discipline*, Peter Senge talks about another's 'fellowship' as a key support for learning, but I think 'family' is a better 'f' word to capture the spirit of partnership. Fellowship could be simply an association, but 'family' implies a much deeper relationship. Learning requires risk taking and experimentation. It necessitates error and mistake. It is uniquely difficult for a mentor to carry out an insight goal (fostering discovery) from an in-charge (I'm the boss) role. Even if the mentor is not in a functional managerial role, simply being an 'expert' creates the potential of unequal power. Applied to mentor and protege, 'family' implies a close relationship, not a parent-child relationship. The goal is partnership.

Freedom

The ultimate test of the expansiveness of the mentoring relationship is when the learner is set free. Mentoring relationships are exercises in ceaseless letting go.

Few conditions do a greater disservice to the protégé than mentor dependence. Dependence leads to protégé uncertainty and insecurity. Dependence results in a relationship that is inefficient and barren of worth to either mentor or protégé. Dependence implies the mentor is the sole repository of the wisdom required by the protégé.

Engendering freedom is all about creating strength and courage. Fostering freedom is also about building bridges to other resources, including linking the protégé up with other mentors. It means helping the protégé connect with a storehouse of resources to be accessed as needed.

SAGE: THE MODEL FOR GREAT MENTORING

If the aim is to nurture 'mastering' — through a mentoring partnership focused on learner discovery and independence, in a climate that reduces boundaries and encourages risk — what are the steps or stages needed to reach that aim?

The mentoring model found in this book is built around the belief that great mentoring requires four core competencies, each of which can be applied in many ways. These competencies form the sequential steps in the process of mentoring. All four have been selected for their ability to blend effectively with. Not accidentally, the first letters of these four competencies (and steps) spell the word SAGE — a helpful mnemonic as well as a symbolic representation of the goal, the power-free facilitation of learning. They are:

> **S**urrendering — leveling the learning field,
> **A**ccepting — creating a safe haven for risk taking,
> **G**ifting — the main event, and
> **E**xtending — nurturing protégé independence.

Surrendering

Most leaders are socially conditioned to *drive* the process of learning; great mentors *surrender* to it. Driving the process has many unfortunate effects. It tends to cause resistance; it minimizes the potential for serendipitous growth, and it tilts the focus from competence to control.

If there is one word many leaders hate, it is the word 'surrender.' However, by 'surrender' I don't mean losing, but yielding to a flow greater than either player in the process. The dictionary defines 'surrender' as "to yield possession of." Mentors who attempt to hold, own, or control the process deprive their protégés of the freedom needed to foster discovery.

Surrendering is the process of leveling the learning field. Most mentoring relationships begin with mentor and protégé in unequal power positions . . . boss to subordinate, master to novice, or teacher to student. The risk is that power creates anxiety and anxiety minimizes risk taking—that ever important ingredient required for growth. Surrendering encompasses all the actions the mentor takes to pull power and authority out of the mentoring relationship so protégé anxiety is lowered and courage is heightened.

Accepting

Accepting is the act of inclusion. Acceptance is what psychologist Carl Rogers labeled "unconditional positive regard." Most managers are taught to focus on exclusion. Exclusion is associated with preferential treatment, presumption, arrogance, and insolence — growth killers all. The verb 'accept,' however, implies ridding oneself of bias, preconceived judgments, and human labeling. Accepting is embracing, rather than evaluating or judging.

Accepting is code for creating a safe haven for learning. When mentors demonstrate noticeable curiosity, they telegraph acceptance. When mentors encourage and support, they send a message that safety abounds. Protégés need safety in the mentoring relationship in order to undertake experimental behavior in the face of public vulnerability.

> "The first problem for all of us, men and women, is not to learn, but to unlearn."
> — Gloria Steinem

Gifting

Gifting is the act of generosity. Gifting, as opposed to giving, means bestowing something of value upon another without expecting anything in return. Mentors have many gifts to share. When they bestow those gifts abundantly and unconditionally, they strengthen the relationship and keep it healthy. Gifting is the antithesis of taking or using manipulatively. It is at the opposite end of the spectrum from greed.

Gifting is often seen as the main event of mentoring. Mentors *give* advice; they *give* feedback; they *give* focus and direction, they *give* proper balance between intervening and letting protégés test their wings, and they *give* their passion for learning. However, just as we all recoil at the sound of 'Let me give you some advice,' protégés must be ready for the mentor's gifts. Surrendering and accepting are important initial steps in creating a readiness in the protégé. Gifts are wasted when they are not valued — when they are discounted and discarded.

Extending

Extending means pushing the relationship beyond its expected boundaries. Mentors who extend are those willing to give up the relationship in the interest of growth, to seek alternative ways to foster growth. They recognize that the protégé's learning can occur and be enhanced in many and mysterious ways. Extending is needed to create an independent self-directed learner.

Surrendering, accepting, gifting, and extending are the capabilities or proficiencies required for the mentor to be an effective partner in the protégé's growth. These four core competencies also serve as the organizing structure for the rest of this book. Their sequence is important. The process of mentoring begins with surrendering and ends with extending. Under each of the four competencies you will find several chapters full of techniques for demonstrating that competence effectively.

Mentoring is an honor. Except for love, there is no greater gift one can give another than the gift of growth. It is a rare privilege to help another learn, have the relevant wisdom be useful to another, and partner with someone who can benefit from that wisdom. This book is crafted with a single goal: to help you exercise that honor and privilege in a manner that benefits you and all those you influence.

CHAPTER 2
Mentoring in Action
A CONTINUING CASE

Jack Gamble was the consummate outdoorsman. Every deer, dove, quail, turkey, and largemouth bass was in grave danger whenever Jack entered the wild with his rifle, shotgun, bow, or reel. But at Gracie-Omar, Inc., he was the consummate mentor. Jack was the manufacturing engineering manager at the Triplin, Georgia, plant of Gracie-Omar, a large computer systems and components plant.

He had done his time in the trenches and had quickly worked his way up the chain. Now he reported directly to the plant manager. Jack's upward mobility was due not only to his superior performance and down-home humor but to his unique way of communicating to associates what he learned. As the plant expanded, the plant manager promoted Jack repeatedly, seeing him as the prototype of a 'learning organization leader.'

Tracy Black was a new systems engineer transferred to Gracie-Omar's Triplin plant from their plant north of Boston. Tracy would ultimately be assigned to Jack and had nothing in common with him, except hunting. Tracy was from upstate New York; Jack was local, born and raised twenty-five miles from Triplin. Tracy had a somber and clipped style; Jack had a mile-wide smile and a drawl as slow as molasses. Tracy was a liberal Republican and Catholic; Jack was a deacon in the Baptist church and a conservative Democrat. Not least, Tracy was a woman; Jack was not.

Tracy and Jack first met at the company picnic. It was Tracy's second day. She arrived thirty minutes late. The only people she knew were the human resources director who had interviewed her, and Rod, the plant manager, whom she had briefly met. The crowd seemed very cliquish to her, their boisterous conversation like code: 'We're all big buddies here, and if you're not one of us now, you won't be in this lifetime!' The meeting planner announced how the meal would be served, the plant manager made a short speech, and Jack told a long joke about a mule. The crowd laughed and cheered; she didn't understand what was funny about the punch line. She thought of Boston.

"Howdy," said someone behind her as she was reaching for a short ear of corn in a long serving line. Startled, she quickly turned. "I'm Jack Gamble. Rod tells me you and I will be working together."

Oh, no! she thought privately, Not the mule man! But she managed to utter a crisp "Hello."

Jack asked her the usual fair-weather, cocktail-party questions — where ya from, where'd ya go to school, what'd ya do before you came here, ya wanna sit? At the end of five minutes, Jack suggested that Tracy stop by his office on Monday right after lunch.

Jack's office revealed few clues about its occupant. As Tracy waited there for him to return from a luncheon meeting, she searched for clues about this man who would be her boss and mentor. On the desk was a picture of Jack's wife and two children; on the wall, a framed ISO-9000 certificate and a picture of two wild turkeys. On the floor behind the desk was a piece of equipment that looked like a large blue jug. Other than that, the office could have belonged to anyone.

"Sorry I'm late!" she heard from behind her. "Would ya like a glass of real good homemade iced tea?" he asked with the same impish style he had used to tell the mule joke.

"No," said Tracy, more brusquely than she had intended.

Jack served himself from the large blue jug. He turned around as he began speaking, warmth and confidence in his words. "Tracy, I'm real excited about getting to work with you. Sarah, over in human resources, tells me you are one terrific systems engineer." Tracy didn't know how to respond, but Jack continued, not seeming to want a response from her yet. "You've worked on the LWB-211, which I would really like to know more about. We haven't gotten any of those in here yet, but we plan to in the fourth quarter.

"Now, how can I help you get settled in?" Tracy was not sure, but she asked Jack whether she would be getting a laptop with a high speed modem that would enable her to link into the company intranet when she worked on the road.

"That's a new one," said Jack, writing it on a small pad. "I'll find out and let you know right away. I've been keeping a list of the questions new people ask, along with the answers. I've made you a copy. But the modem question won't be in this issue!" Tracy was beginning to feel more comfortable with Jack.

"I don't know what you think of this plant," Jack went on, "but I sure do remember what I felt at first. It seemed like a tight family that didn't want any more cousins! I remember feeling downright scared and wondering if I'd made a bum decision. But I made up my mind I wasn't going to let it beat me. I just started acting like I was already in the family. And you know what? It worked like a thirty-ought-six on an eight-pointer at twenty yards!"

Tracy was surprised. "You're a hunter?" she asked.

Jack's eyes twinkled mischievously. He looked like someone who had been caught with his hand in the cookie jar. "You bet!" he said. "And if you aren't, then I just messed in my nest — using an expression that only another hunter would get."

"I hunt, too," replied Tracy, somewhat relieved to have one thing in common with this slow-talking foreigner.

"Terrific!" said Jack. "Do you like to hunt deer?"

Tracy nodded. "I hunt anything in season," she said. It was her first foray into Southern mores.

Jack leaned forward. "That's great! Have you seen the new issue of Field and Stream? She had not. "Well, I have it right here. Why don't you take it? There's a great article on deer stands — has some crazy ideas I plan to try next time my son and I go deer hunting." Tracy began to loosen up as they continued to talk for some time on their newfound common interest.

A few weeks after Jack and Tracy's get-acquainted meeting, an Ulmer-1911 machine was delivered. Jack had been Ulmer-qualified for a few years and had gone back to Wisconsin twice for refresher training. Tracy had heard about but never operated the machine and was eager to learn. Late one afternoon Jack and Tracy sat down for the first time at the console of the 1911.

"Before we start," Jack began, "I want to find out what you know about this machine." He listened as Tracy described the machine's purpose and what it could produce. "I see you've done your homework," he said proudly. Tracy smiled.

Jack continued: "Think of this machine as an extension of your right arm and imagine what it would feel like to have that arm ten feet longer than the other. Not only does hand-eye coordination change, but you're bound to feel awkward. Expect that same sensation with the Ulmer-1911."

Tracy began to feel a bit less apprehensive. "Are you going to show me how it works?" she asked, her impatience beginning to show.

"I was just like you," Jack teased, "as anxious as a long-tailed cat in a room full of rocking chairs." Tracy grinned and took a deep breath. "But," Jack continued, "it will be better for you to run this machine than to watch me run it. Just looking at the center screen, what do you think is the first step?"

Tracy quickly responded, "I'd say keying on command six and moving the dugen switch to ninety degrees."

"Great choice!" Jack answered. "And what's your objective in taking that route?"

The lesson continued until Tracy was operating the Ulmer fairly proficiently. The only time Jack touched the equipment was after Tracy had taken a series of incorrect steps and gotten so far off the starting point that she needed help getting back. Jack's goal was to guide her thinking and understanding more than her operating and remembering.

In the months that followed, Jack and Tracy's relationship improved. Their mutual interest in hunting turned out to be a key source of compatibility. As Tracy grew less nervous and more confident, she began to take more risks in her spirited interaction with Jack. Soon she was matching him jab for friendly jab. She also began assuming greater plant responsibility, including the supervision of four engineers.

One day she stopped Jack in the hall with a look of concern on her face. "Got a few minutes?" she asked.

Five minutes later they were in her office. "Adam's a problem," she began bluntly after Jack closed the door behind him.

She had learned that with Jack there was no need to beat around the bush. "Just cut to the chase," he had encouraged her. It had proven helpful in her dealings with some of the more impatient engineers.

"Tell me more," Jack replied, sitting in the chair in front of her desk.

Adam was one of Tracy's new direct reports. "He's not pulling his weight. I've encouraged him, counseled him, and tried to understand him. I'm running out of patience."

Jack waited to make sure she had no more to say about the subject. "How can I help?" he asked, not wanting to assume anything yet about whether his assistance was required.

Tracy looked straight at him. "I guess I need you to be a sounding board, and maybe give me some ideas on how to get him fired up — or fired."

"What do you think the problem is, based on what you know?" asked Jack.

"His morale is lousy. When I try to talk with him about his performance, his nonverbals are rather patronizing, like he's offended that I raised the issue."

Jack thought for a minute. "I can see that would be a tough nut to crack. I've never been really comfortable dealing with negative performers. It always makes me feel anxious if I have to get tough with an employee. I can see — "

"But you still manage to get them turned around," interrupted Tracy.

Jack could see that Tracy thought he had some magical secret he had kept to himself. "You believe there's a special technique that maybe you've missed."

"Yes, I suppose I do, in a way. You make it look easy. I remember when you had to terminate Edsel Joiner. The guy ended up thanking you for it!"

Jack did not respond for a while. Tracy suddenly felt awkward, as though she had allowed her stream of emotion to overflow its banks. Then, with unusual emotion in his voice, Jack said, "That was the scariest thing I've ever done since I came to work here." They both sat in silence.

Jack took another stab at the issue. "How does he react when you get stern and serious?"

"I'm not sure," Tracy responded.

Jack tried again. "Let me ask it this way: If I asked Adam to candidly describe you when the two of you talk about his performance, what words would he use?"

Tracy's demeanor began to change. It was as if the wheels of wisdom were turning in her head.

"He would say I was relentlessly patient." She was still half lost in thought.

"What else?"

Tracy responded with near excitement in her voice. "He would not describe me as tough, demanding, or disciplined."

Jack sensed that she was solving her own issue. Again, he paused before raising another question. He knew instinctively that pace was everything when insight was the goal. "So, what do you think should be your next step?"

Tracy began to outline steps: a serious conversation, a performance plan, short-term goals with clear feedback, supervision with a shorter leash, and, above all, less understanding and more discipline. Jack offered a few ideas, but mostly affirmation and encouragement. They parted with an agreement to revisit the issue in a few days.

The story had a happy ending. Adam admitted to Tracy that he was having difficulty working for a woman, but ultimately grew to respect her, turning out excellent performance. Tracy was promoted to department manager, and then transferred to corporate headquarters in Wisconsin. Jack mentored more new engineers. He was offered promotions but turned down any that involved a move. Woods for hunting were more important than mahogany row. Besides, he got a kick out watching people learn — especially those who weren't sure they were going to fit in.

> "A successful career will no longer be about promotion. It will be about mastery."
> — Michael Hammer

CHAPTER 3
Assessing Your Mentoring Talents
A SELF-CHECK SCALE

Self-assessment: Does the term make you think of navel gazing? Perhaps you've had enough of the joys of testing, performance reviews, exams, and the like. For many, testing feels more about masochism than mastery! However, drawing a finer bead on our gifts and blind spots is a precursor to improvement and growth — and that, after all, is what mentoring is all about.

The Mentor Scale is a painless way to determine what personal attributes you bring to the mentoring relationship. The goal is not to judge, evaluate, or criticize you as a person; there are no right or wrong answers. The objective is to offer you a picture of your gifts and your potential blind spots. For example, if I know I have a tendency to procrastinate, I can take steps to counter that tendency, to break the habit of putting things off until the last minute.

At this point, you may be thinking of zipping past this chapter. Please resist the temptation. I encourage you to work through the self-assessment. There will be many references to it throughout the rest of the book. If you haven't done it, you will miss out on some potentially powerful mentoring insights. You do not have to put your answers in the book; simply write them on a separate sheet of paper. This way you can easily review your answers as we revisit the Mentor Scale at various points throughout the book.

Now, pencil ready? Here goes . . .

THE TEST

The Mentor Scale on the following pages lists thirty-nine sentence stems, each with two possible endings. Keeping your work environment in mind, quickly review each item and circle the letter of the ending that best completes the sentence. Read each item carefully, but choose your response quickly. Instruments like this tend to be more accurate if you go with your immediate reaction rather than pondering your choice. Do not leave items blank. You will find some items in which neither choice is perfectly accurate. Select the one that seems better. After completing the inventory, proceed to the scoring form.

THE MENTOR SCALE

1. People probably see me as   a. hard-nosed   b. a soft touch

2. Work days I like the most are   a. unpredictable   b. planned

3. When it comes to celebrations, most organizations need   a. fewer   b. more

4. When I evaluate people, my decisions are based on   a. justice   b. mercy

5. My approach to planning my personal activities is   a. easygoing   b. orderly

6. People generally see me as a person who is   a. formal   b. personable

7. When it comes to social situations, I tend to   a. hold back   b. jump in

8. I like to spend my leisure time in ways that are fairly   a. spontaneous   b. routine

9. I believe leaders should be more concerned about employee   a. rights   b. feelings

10. When I encounter people in need of help, I'm more likely to   a. avoid   b. pitch in

11. When I am in a group, I typically   a. follow   b. lead

12. Most people see me as   a. private   b. open

13. My friends know that I am   a. firm   b. gentle

14. If I were in a group of strangers, people would most likely remember me as a   a. listener   b. leader

15. When it comes to expressing my feelings, most people probably see me as   a. guarded   b. comfortable

16. When people I depend on make mistakes, I am typically   a. patient   b. impatient

17. When I eat out, I generally order food that   a. sounds unique   b. I know I like

18. In general, I prefer   a. the theater   b. a party

19. In a conflict, when anger is involved, my emotional fuse is usually   a. short   b. long

20. In an emergency situation, I would likely be   a. calm   b. anxious

21. I prefer to express myself to others in ways that are   a. indirect   b. direct

22. I am likely to be ruled by   a. logic   b. emotion

23. When in new and unfamiliar situations, I am usually   a. carefree   b. careful

24. In a festive social situation, I am usually   a. passive   b. active

25. When I am blamed for something I did not cause, my initial reaction is to   a. listen   b. defend

26. If I am in a situation in which I lose or am left disappointed, I get   a. sad   b. mad

27. If someone came to me in tears, I would probably feel   a. awkward   b. at home

28. Most people see me as   a. an optimist   b. a pessimist

29. People usually see me as   a. uncritical   b. critical

30. If people were given a forced
    choice, they would say I was   a. too quiet   b. too loud

31. At the end of long party, I usually
    find myself   a. exhausted   b. energized

32. When I work on projects, I am
    best at getting them   a. started   b. completed

33. I believe people should approach
    their work with   a. dedication   b. inspiration

34. My social blunders typically leave me a. embarrassed b. amused

35. When my organization announces
    a major change, I get   a. excited   b. concerned

36. People are likely to see me as   a. firm   b. warm

37. After a tough day, I like to unwind   a. alone   b. with others

38. Change is most often your.   a. friend   b. adversary

39. My work and social life   a. are separate b. often overlap

"You never find yourself until you face the truth."
— Pearl Bailey

THE SCORING FORM

Sociability

Using simple hatch marks, tally your A's and B's for the thirteen sociability items.

	A's	B's
1, 4, 7, 10, 13, 16, 19, 22, 25, 28, 31, 34, 37 Totals	_____	_____

Dominance

Do the same for the thirteen dominance items . . .

	A's	B's
2, 5, 8, 11, 14, 17, 20, 23, 26, 29, 32, 35, 38 Totals	_____	_____

Openness

. . . and for the thirteen openness items.

	A's	B's
3, 6, 9, 12, 15, 18, 21, 24, 27, 30, 33, 36, 39 Totals	_____	_____

Interpretation

The Mentor Scale is inspired by the FIRO-B®, an excellent instrument developed by Will Schutz and distributed exclusively by Consulting Psychologists Press, Palo Alto, California (650) 969-8901. The scale measures — at one point in time — a mentor's need for sociability, dominance, and openness, all crucial components of an effective mentoring relationship. (Schutz's FIRO-B® instrument labels these components 'inclusion,' 'control,' and 'affection,' respectively.)

Sociability has to do with your preference for being with or apart from others. People with high column-A scores in sociability tend to be reserved loners;

those with high column-B scores tend to be outgoing joiners. People with similar numbers of A's and B's are neither highly sociable nor highly reserved; they can be moderately sociable or moderately reserved, depending on the situation.

What does sociability have to do with mentoring? People who have high sociability scores will find the rapport-building and dialogue-leading dimensions of mentoring easier. They will have to work hard to avoid dominating discussions. Low sociability scores are found among people whose reserve may make them a bit unapproachable. These people will need to work harder at helping protégés open up and communicate.

Dominance is about your preference regarding being in charge. People with high column-A scores are comfortable having someone else do the leading, and often prefer it. People with high column-B scores tend to like being in control and often assert that need. Low dominance scores can also indicate a high need for independence. People with balanced scores are neither highly dominant nor highly submissive. They can control moderately or not at all, depending on the situation.

Dominance is a major issue in mentoring with a partnering philosophy. The whole concept of mentoring today is based on a relationship of shared power. High dominance scorers are reluctant either to give up control or to share control of the relationship; they have to work hard to listen rather than talk. Low dominance scorers, on the other hand, may need to work to assume leadership of the relationship. They may take such a low-key, laissez-faire approach that the protégé feels insecure and without guidance.

Openness refers to how easily you trust others. High column-A scores are found among people who are cautious, guarded, and reluctant to show feelings. High column-B scores are typical of people with many close relationships, who are comfortable being vulnerable and tend to express their feelings easily. People with similar A and B scores are moderately open or moderately cautious, depending on the situation.

High openness scorers will find it easy to reveal themselves in a mentoring relationship. In fact, their challenge is to be candid and open enough to encourage the protégé to do likewise, while not being so aggressive as to overwhelm or intimidate the protégé. Low openness scorers, however, will need to work at overcoming their caution in order to take early emotional and interpersonal risks with the protégé; their instinctive guardedness can make the protégé feel that mistakes might have dire consequences.

Several chapters ahead have sidebars addressing the implications of your Mentor Scale scores in terms of each chapter's issues and challenges. The goal is to show you how to use your strengths and compensate for your weaknesses. Is it possible to be too sociable or too open? Of course! Is it not important in some situations to be highly dominant? Again, of course! For effective mentoring, however, my view is that you push toward the high side of sociability and openness, toward the low side of dominance.

Remember, the Mentor Scale gives you a reading at a moment in time, one that may change with the circumstances. Keep in mind also that the scale assesses only three aspects of your leadership personality. Don't generalize the results beyond their intent; too often, personality instruments are used to label or categorize people, to discount their individual uniqueness. Learn from the Mentor Scale — but avoid using the results as though they were holy writ.

Part II

Surrendering:
LEVELING THE LEARNING FIELD

Surrendering

LEVELING THE LEARNING FIELD

Luke Skywalker is stranded on a strange planet, his spaceship submerged deep in sludge. His only company is his mentor, Yoda, the Jedi warrior. "Use the force," says the tiny, strange-looking creature. "I'll try," replies a discouraged, exhausted Luke. "Try?" retorts Yoda. "There is no try. Either lift it or don't lift it."

All fans of *The Empire Strikes Back* know how this scene ends. After Luke gives up, Yoda, using some strange connection with a universal energy field, wills the spaceship out of the bog and onto dry land. Although this is just movie magic, every person in the theater has a strange identification with Yoda's action.

The force behind Yoda's action goes by many names. An artist refers to it as 'the muse.' Surfers call it 'flow'; dancers call it 'hot,' others call it 'being in the groove' or 'being on.' Call it what you may, the feeling is unmistakable. There is a similar moment in a mentoring relationship when everything clicks and a spirit or force seems to lift the connection to a level of purity, of unspoken understanding. Wisdom, insight, and growth burst from these moments. Learning happens at warp speed. We seem surprisingly clear and uniquely receptive to understanding. This is mentoring at its best.

How does this high-octane learning occur? What action does the mentor need to take to encourage this synergistic moment with a protégé? In a word, surrender. The magical first step is to surrender to the process.

Surrendering means completely relinquishing any effort to control or manipulate the outcome. Surrendering means putting all effort into being completely authentic, real, and mask-free. Surrendering means being devoted to learning, not dedicated to convincing. As management consultant Bruce Fritch says, "Surrendering is the most difficult and most courageous interpersonal act a leader can take with a subordinate. It is also the most powerful!"

Mentors surrender in several ways. One of these could be called 'mask removal' — the willingness to be open and vulnerable. We all wear masks, in part to protect ourselves against rejection. When a mentor removes this mask in front of the protégé, it changes the nature of the relationship from cautious to unguarded. Energy normally devoted to cover and protection becomes available for insight and discovery.

Years ago I worked with Dr. Richard Furr, a gifted consulting psychologist. He and I designed and taught a series of executive workshops on performance coaching. The final advice Richard gave attendees was to practice their newfound skills on a couple of subordinates within the coming week: "Start with practice, by telling your associates something like the following: 'I have just attended a workshop on performance coaching and learned some new skills I want to use in our relationship. I will be very awkward at first and make a lot of mistakes. But with some practice and your patience, I will get better. And we will both benefit.'"

The advice was a valuable relationship builder. Attendees at follow-up sessions reported enormous success. The authenticity caused subordinates to see their leaders in a new light. Many reported that their sessions with subordinates turned out to be the single most powerful and productive conversation they had ever had. The typical executive report went something like this: 'When I gave up trying to force it to work, it seemed to take on a life of its on and steered the relationship where it needed to go. It was amazing. I have never felt anything like it. It was like magic.' This like-magic quality of mentoring begins to happen with surrendering.

Surrendering is fundamentally about being assertively honest and candid, with the intention of helping, not hurting, the other person. There is a cleanness and frankness about relationships in which authenticity is valued. Great mentors care enough to be honest and forthright; they are also curious and learning oriented enough to invite and accept candor from the protégé.

CHAPTER 4
Kindling Kinship
THE POWER OF RAPPORT

Rapport comes from an old French word that means 'a bringing back' or 'harmony renewed.' This definition reminds us that rapport is fundamentally about actions aimed at restoring the security of the bond with which we begin life: infant and mother. Life, for most of us, does not start with anxiety or fear. Life begins with security and trust. The path from dependence to independence teaches us about rejection, discomfort, and pain. We protect ourselves with the shield of personality (the Greek word for 'personality' means 'mask') and assume that each new relationship is a threat until shown otherwise. The ritual of relationship is the gradual lowering of the mask.

The success of a mentoring relationship can hang on the first encounters between mentor and protégé. The tone set in the first meeting can determine whether the relationship will be fruitful or fraught with fear and anxiety. Rapport building expedites shield lowering; quality learning will not occur until the shield has been lowered enough for the learner to take risks in front of the mentor. As the person who is usually in the driver's seat at the outset of the relationship, the mentor must ensure a good start — the renewal of the original bond.

Can a mentoring relationship get back on track if the first encounter falters? Of course — and thank goodness. Most of us can remember a solid friendship that started out on shaky ground. We also remember how long it took and how much energy had to be expended to overcome that rocky beginning. But the sooner we can establish rapport, the more time and energy we save — and the sooner the relationship moves onto solid ground, the faster learning can occur. The old Southern customs of bringing a gift when visiting a friend, telling a funny story to open a speech, or making small talk to kick off a sales call all acknowledge that openings are potentially rocky *and* important.

THE COMPONENTS OF RAPPORT

What does rapport building entail for a mentor? How does the mentor establish early kinship, trust, and comfort? What follows is a discussion of the four components of rapport: leveling communications, gifting gestures, receptivity for feel-

ings, and reflective responses. (Okay, there are probably twenty-five components
— or twenty-five hundred — but in this book we will work with four. We all know
there is not a finite number of most things, especially in areas like habits, wonders
of the world, ways to leave your lover, or components of rapport. The four here
were chosen for convenience and workability.) The point is, develop your own
techniques for rapport building, consistent with the spirit of these components.
To jump start your efforts, I've included several applications in each section.

Leveling Communication

Rapport begins with the sounds and sights of openness and positive regard. Any
normal person approaching a potentially anxious encounter will raise his antennae
high in search of clues about the road ahead: Will this situation embarrass me? Will
this person take advantage of me? Will I be effective in this encounter? Is there harm
awaiting me?

Given the protégé's search for early warning signs, the mentor must be quick
to transmit signals of welcome. An open posture (for example, no crossed arms),
warm and enthusiastic gestures, eye contact, removing physical barriers, and personalized greetings all communicate a desire for a level playing field. Mentors
who broadcast power signals (peering over an imposing desk, making the protégé
do all the approaching, tight and closed body language, a reserved manner, or facial expressions that telegraph distance) risk complete failure to establish a good
mentoring partnership.

Gifting Gestures

The opening communication can signal only that the path ahead may be safe
for travel; it does not ensure rapport. The 'Actions speak louder than words' adage
is uniquely fitting at this juncture. Protégés need a gesture or action that they can
take as a token of affinity.

Establishing rapport is a bit like courtship. You don't say, 'Hi, I'm Bill. Let's
get married. How's tomorrow at three?' There are the little matters of dating, gifts,
parties, meeting the family, showers, ministers — all the preliminaries needed for
a long-lasting and rewarding relationship.

The best mentors are especially creative with these signals. The perfunctory
'How about a cup of coffee?' is certainly a well-worn gifting gesture. However,
think about how much more powerful a statement like 'I had my assistant locate

this article I thought you might find useful' could be as early evidence that the relationship will be a friendly one. I once had a mentor who kept a supply of his wife's homemade jellies for visitors. The gift was always bestowed early in the encounter, not at the end.

There are as many ways to signal benign intent as there are mentors and protégés. Find one that suits you and works for your associates.

Receptivity for Feelings

The great psychologist Carl Rogers wrote extensively on unconditional positive regard and its impact on relationships. His research repeatedly affirmed the role such a generous attitude has on psychological healing and wellness. A good mentor establishes rapport through careful attentiveness to the protégé's feelings early in the encounter. When people believe they are heard and understood, they feel secure and comfortable. Establishing rapport is not about asking, 'How are you feeling?' It is about listening intently to ascertain the feelings behind the words — and (as we will see in chapter 11) making responses that acknowledge these feelings.

In her article "What Exactly Is Charisma?" Patricia Sellers profiles Orit Gadiesh, the former chair of the prestigious consulting firm Bain & Company: "Orit has that talent for making you feel you're the most important person in the room. She bleeds your blood." One way she makes clients feel important, reports Sellers, is by never looking at her watch. Inside Bain, Gadiesh was regarded as a junior consultant's most generous mentor.

In her story "Mockingbirds," Mary Oliver tells of an elderly couple visited by strangers in their poor abode. Lacking any goods to offer their visitors, the couple simply listens to their guests with all their heart. The strangers turn out to be gods who view the couple's attentiveness as the very best gift humans can give. Gods and protégés are moved and mellowed by mentors who listen from the heart. As a mentor, continually ask yourself, 'What must he or she be feeling right now? How might I feel if our roles were reversed?'

Reflective Responses

Receptivity to the protégé's feelings enables you to provide a tailor-made reflective response that says, 'I've been there as well.' This gesture, another way of saying, 'I am similar to you,' promotes the kinship and closeness that are vital to trust. The goal is empathetic identification. Empathy is different from sympathy. The word 'sympathy' comes from the Greek word synpatheia, meaning 'shared feeling.' Empathy means 'in-feeling,' or the ability to understand another's feelings. Relationship strength is not spawned by 'Misery loves company'; it comes through 'I've been there too' identification.

Reflective responses can be as simple as a short personal story that lets the protégé know that you appreciate his feelings. Mildly self-deprecating anecdotes can work well, too. Above all, rapport is best served by humility and sensitivity. If you feel awkward, say you do. If you feel excited, say so. The sooner you speak your feelings, the faster the protégé will match your vulnerability.

These ideas about rapport are meant to spark your thinking seriously about how to begin this important getting-started phase of mentoring. However, you should also keep in mind that the main ingredient in the recipe for rapport is authenticity. The more you surrender to who you are in front of the protégé, the more at home she will feel. Compatibility is as vital in mentoring as in any other important relationship. How quickly and effectively that compatibility is established can make a major difference in how competent the protégé becomes.

Jack Gamble on Rapport
(Mentoring In Action Revisited)

"Sorry I'm late!" she heard from behind her. "Would ya like a glass of real good homemade iced tea?" he asked with the same impish style he had used to tell the mule joke.

"No," said Tracy, more brusquely than she had intended.

Jack served himself from the large blue jug. He turned as he began speaking, warmth and confidence in his words. "Tracy, I'm real excited about getting to work with you. Sarah, over in human resources, tells me you are one terrific systems engineer." Tracy didn't know how to respond, but Jack continued, not seeming to want a response from her yet. "You've worked on the LWB-211, which I would really like to know more about. We haven't gotten any of those in here yet, but we plan to in the fourth quarter.

"Now, how can I help you get settled in?" Tracy was not sure, but she asked Jack whether she would be getting a laptop with a high speed modem that would enable her to link into the company intranet when she worked on the road.

"That's a new one," said Jack, writing it on a small pad. "I'll find out and let you know right away. I've been keeping a list of the questions new people ask, along with the answers. I've made you a copy. But the modem question won't be in this issue!" Tracy was beginning to feel more comfortable with Jack.

"I don't know what you think of this plant," Jack went on, "but I sure do remember what I felt at first. It seemed like a tight family that didn't want any more cousins! I remember feeling downright scared and wondering if I'd made a bum decision. But I made up my mind I wasn't going to let it beat me. I just started acting like I was already in the family. And you know what? It worked like a thirty-ought-six on an eight-pointer at twenty yards!"

Tracy was surprised. "You're a hunter?" she asked.

Jack's eyes twinkled mischievously. He looked like someone who had been caught with his hand in the cookie jar. "You bet!" he said. "And if you aren't, then I just messed in my nest — using an expression that only another hunter would get."

"I hunt, too," replied Tracy, somewhat relieved to have one thing in common with this slow-talking foreigner.

"Terrific!" said Jack. "Do you like to hunt deer?"

Tracy nodded. "I hunt anything in season," she said. It was her first foray into Southern mores.

Jack leaned forward. "That's great! Have you seen the new issue of Field and Stream? She had not. "Well, I have it right here. Why don't you take it? There's a great article on deer stands — has some crazy ideas I plan to try next time my son and I go deer hunting." Tracy began to loosen up as they continued to talk for some time on their newfound common interest.

◼

"Real education consists of drawing the best out of yourself."

— Mohandas Gandhi

CHAPTER 5

The Elements of Trust Making

"THIS COULD BE THE START OF SOMETHING BIG"

n Monday, October 30, 2000, Stephen Valentine Patrick William Allen died of an apparent heart attack at age 78 while napping at his son's home in Encino, California. The author of more than fifty books and five thousand songs, Steve Allen was regarded as the founding father of the late-night talk show. The world knew him as an accomplished comedian, talented musician and innovative talk show host. But to the countless entertainers privileged to have been understudies to Allen — Andy Williams, Steve Lawrence, Eydie Gorme, Steve Martin, Billy Crystal, Don Knotts, and Bill Dana — he was the consummate mentor.

The night following his death Larry King did a CNN special segment on the great Steve Allen. Admirers like Ed McMahon, Carl Reiner, Steve Lawrence, and Mike Douglas were on the show. Call-ins included Don Rickles and Andy Williams. Other interviews in print and on the air in the days that followed added to the epitaph crafted by King's guests by revealing the reason for Allen's huge fan club of entertainment greats. Allen mentored them all with trust.

Trust is a crucial commodity throughout a mentoring relationship. In fact research shows that even if the mentor has terrific interpersonal skills they count for naught without a high level of trust. Conversely, a mentor with only modest mentoring skills can be successful if the protégé experiences a high level of trust. But what is the nature of trust? If trust were something you could reverse engineer, what parts would you find inside?

My partner Ron Zemke has been conducting extensive research into the elements that result in trust in relationships. While his focus has been on coaching, the elements apply to almost every interpersonal alliance. Trust, according to Zemke, is a blend of authenticity (genuiness), credibility (reliability), and communication.

COMMUNICATING GENUINENESS, ALLEN-STYLE

Trust starts with authenticity. We trust another when we perceive his or her motives to be genuine or credible. And Steve Allen was always real! His assertive authenticity quickly calmed even the most uptight star-in-the-making. On one famous sketch on the forerunner of *The Tonight Show*, Allen got tickled at his own joke. The more he laughed, the more tickled he became. Instead of stopping to regain his composure, he simply let his honest giggle attack run rampant. It was unadulterated authenticity, expressed out loud. It counts among the funniest sketches in television history.

Although one of the most brilliant comedians in entertainment history, Allen always seemed awed by his capacity. He seemed so busy looking ahead at what he could be that he gave no time to gloating over what he had been. His fans and protégés say that his coaching conversations were more joint exploration than boasting exhibitions.

You're not a Steve Allen, you say? No matter. There are many ways you can demonstrate authenticity, especially at the beginning of the mentoring session. Start with a pleasant facial expression. Greet your protégé like you are sincerely glad to see him or her. Communicate your enthusiasm for the privilege of mentoring and what it can mean for both of you. Look for a way to provide an early honest compliment. And always remember two things: Be completely honest, and never communicate in a manner that might be perceived by your protégé as patronizing. 'You have a great reputation for being an enthusiastic learner' can be much more powerful way to start building trust than 'That sure is a handsome briefcase.'

If you are feeling a bit anxious, say so — but in a fashion that helps build a bond. 'I'm a bit overwhelmed by this mentoring assignment . . . but, at the same time I'm excited about what we can accomplish together' is much preferred to 'I'm really nervous, are you?' Reveal something personal about yourself, especially something that your protégé may not know and that could provide insight into who you are. 'I'm kind of a private person, and I may seem a bit hard to get to know at first' is much better than 'I like baseball, Pabst Blue Ribbon® beer, and people who tell me what's on their mind. How about you?'

COMMUNICATING CREDIBILITY, ALLEN-STYLE

Trust depends on credibility. We trust another when we believe the person has the wherewithal to actually perform what is promised or needed. Wherewithal includes competence, credentials, and correct conduct. We examine the plaques on the physician's wall, see the badge on the police officer's uniform, or hear the tone of the pilot's voice during in-flight turbulence to gain clues into matters of credibility.

Allen was great at demonstrating credibility as a step in trust building. 'What if we did it like this?' prefaced his lessons in stage performance. His tone carried three essential ingredients for communicating credibility: exposition, exploration, and inclusion. Allen knew how to show off without being a show-off. His display revealed the edge of his enormous talent in a fashion that gave his protégé a kind of 'this guy is really good' confidence in him without unleashing an intimidating internal reaction of 'I could never do that.' His lessons were 'we' lessons, as in 'a smart person mentoring a smart person.' "He was always willing to share what he knew," said Ed McMahon, "as if it was yours all along and he was simply returning something he had borrowed."

How does a mentor communicate credibility without alienating or intimidating the protégé? Credibility needs to fit the context, and the mentoring context is one of support and partnership. A boxing coach might gain credibility with a demeanor as clipped and gruff as an upper cut. The credibility context for a surgeon might be more factual than illustrative, grounded more in technique than in rapport. But in the business world, credibility is best expressed more subtly — in the way one might add a pinch of salt to a bland dish. Credibility should enter the relationship as if somehow invited by the protégé, not sent by the mentor.

Tell a personal story that uses your expertise as the backdrop, not the subject. 'When I was helping Jack Welch craft his strategic plan, we faced the dilemma of how to get the enthusiastic endorsement of the union....' Preface an affirmation with a tidbit from your resume. 'Your new role sounds as exciting as the regional VP slot I had in South Africa in eighty-eight!' Share a take-away that benefits the protégé but trumpets your competence or eligibility. 'You might find this article I wrote for *Harvard Business Review* helpful in explaining some of the craziness of this industry.' Ask questions that reveal expertise...but never in a testing manner or arrogant fashion. Remember, credibility is a tool for trust — your protégé's trust! Consider your exposition of your talents from the perspective of what your protégé needs, not what you need.

COMMUNICATING ANYTHING, ALLEN-STYLE

Zemke's research indicates trust comes in part through communication that contains two features: *task* (underscore precision and authority) and *personal* (emphasis on empathy and consideration). When someone speaks with noticeable authority and crystal clarity, our trust meter goes up. When someone tries to communicate with us with our welfare obviously in mind, she or he gains our confidence. Interpersonal trust is by definition both personal and interpersonal — as in 'between persons.' And the link we have between persons is our manner of communication.

Steve Allen was a master at both aspects of trust-building communication. His booming voice could be heard across a crowded party. And being well over six feet tall didn't hurt his projection prowess. But it was his purity of purpose that latch-keyed attention. "He was a man who spoke with conviction," said his protégé Andy Williams. "When he spoke, people listened because he not only knew what he was talking about, he *sounded* like he knew what he was talking about." When he invited his audiences to give him a subject on which he would craft a song on the spot, he got plenty of volunteers. Audiences knew that his confident requests not only telegraphed his assurance but also would lead to their amusement, not to feeding his arrogance.

When you talk with your protégé think of it as trust-building communication that increases in cost with each nonessential word you use . . . verbosity is expensive; brevity is cost effective. Focus on being precise and particular. That's the task element in gaining trust. But here is the equally important part: As you subtract syllables, add expressions of kindness. Trust is just as much about communicating sincere interest in your protégé as it is about scrupulous attention to clarity.

When offering advice or feedback, keep your suggestions crisp and obvious; speak with the confidence of your experience. When getting feedback from your protégé, be quickly appreciative and bold in unearthing additional learning; show confidence in your ability to transform even negative observations into an opportunity for growth. 'But what about humility?' you may ask. Humility and confidence are equal partners in engendering trust. Mentors don't have to hang their heads and stammer to make humility sincere. An unassuming nature means communicating plainly without adding our own agenda. It is the centeredness a sage might communicate to a student, the peacefulness a tutor might convey to a new pupil.

> "Most of the advice we receive from others is not so much evidence of their affection for us, as it is evidence of their affection for themselves."
> — Josh Billings

Steve Allen's genius lies not in the archives of his many TV sketches or the books and music that line library walls. It lives on in the many famous entertainers who reflect his tutelage. When Andy Williams croons Moon River, or scaredy-cat Don Knotts stammers, "But, but, but, Andy . . . ," or Steve and Eydie sing, "Our love is here to stay," a little bit of Steve Allen shines through. And mentors who learn to build trust Allen-style are likewise blessed by his legacy.

CHAPTER 6
Putting the 'us' in Trust
BLENDING HUMILITY WITH CONFIDENCE

The most famous car in Charlotte, North Carolina, in 1971 was a perfectly restored antique Mercedes-Benz sports car owned and driven daily by Luther Hodges, Jr. Luther was then chairman of the board of North Carolina National Bank and the son of a former North Carolina governor and Kennedy administration cabinet member. Tall, handsome, and Harvard educated, Luther was an impressive leader. Coupled with The Car, he was just plain impressive!

I had been with the bank only a few months and considered myself to be about 347 levels below Luther. My occasional meetings with him were always cordial, warm, and upbeat. He went out of his way to help soothe my too-obvious nervousness at being in the presence of the chairman. I wanted to learn from him — and he clearly afforded me the opportunity. However, the emotional space between us felt too wide for me. I picked my words carefully in his presence. Learning from Mr. Hodges always took a back seat to impressing Mr. Hodges. That is, until The Car changed everything.

I was accompanying Luther and my boss to a meeting in Raleigh, about three hours from Charlotte, the city where

> "I bid him look into the lives of men as though into a mirror, and from others to take an example for himself."
> — Terence (190–159 B.C.)

we all lived and worked. My boss and I had driven there in the company Ford checked out in his name only. Luther had driven there in The Car. Our meeting ran late, so Luther and my boss decided to stay over and drive back together early the next morning so they could talk on the drive. Two small problems remained: How was I going to get back to Charlotte that evening, and how was The Car going to get back to Charlotte?

"Chip, why don't you take my car home with you?" suggested Luther, flashing his Steinway smile. "Drive into work in the morning, park in my spot, and just leave the keys with Pam. I'll give you a ride home tomorrow afternoon." My ears rang, my heart pounded, and I was unable to speak for what seemed an eternity. The *chairman* wanted me to drive The Car to my home! He trusted me with his most prized possession! The distance between us evaporated; suddenly I felt that Luther was my friend. My anxiety was magically transformed into confidence and — although I didn't know it at the time — that marked the beginning of my real learning.

Mentoring partnerships work only when there is trust. And trust comes in part from the communication of humility. Luther was as open and trusting as they come. Equally important, his showing authenticity fostered my courage to do likewise. Humility has a special role in relationships in which there is an unequal distribution of power: Trust is the equalizer.

PUT THE PROTÉGÉ ON THE RIGHT

At an early age I learned in school and church that sitting on the right was a special privilege. The Bible makes many references to "sitting at the right hand of God." Kings put their most important ally on their right when attending a banquet. Years later I learned the origin of this custom. Like people in general, most kings (and writers of scripture) were right-handed. In the era of sword and dagger, the right side was the hardest for a right-handed person to defend. To unsheathe a sword with the right hand and strike to the near right was a very awkward move. So the king invited the person he trusted most to sit at his most vulnerable side. It became a station of honor.

The counterpart to putting the protégé on your right is any action that deliberately, as well as symbolically, communicates trust and honor. Luther let me drive home The Car. Now that I'm on the other side of fifty, I'm a bit embarrassed to remember how I felt; it seems juvenile and immature. But if I roll my life story back twenty-five years and reflect on the experience, I remember having the same feeling I had at age ten when my dad told me to go get the tractor and park it in the barn.

The most effective sitting-on-the-right actions are those tailored to the individual. They dramatically demonstrate two aspects of the relationship: a deep understanding of the individual and a recognition that trust is created through trustful actions. A friend of mine remembers when his mentor sent him to an important meeting in his place. A consulting partner describes a time when a giant in his field was unable to keep an engagement and recommended him as his replacement. A boss of mine, unexpectedly called out of the country, asked me to interview a candidate for a very senior position in the company and offered the use of his executive-suite office for the interview. Gestures like these communicate a special trust.

DEMONSTRATE HUMILITY SQUARED

Johnson & Johnson, one of the most trusted organizations in the world today, enhanced their reputation during their darkest hour, the Tylenol® poisoning incident. Instead of covering up the problem or making excuses, the company spent over $100 million to remove every bottle of Tylenol® from shelves around the world. Though the incident proved to be the result of sabotage, J&J assumed responsibility for it — and gained enormous respect and renewed trust from consumers. Actor Hugh Grant's reputation suffered only a slight blip from his escapade with a prostitute because, rather than ducking the press or denying the charges, he went on *Larry King Live*, acknowledged his 'sins,' and asked for the public's forgiveness.

All relationships experience hiccups and less-than-perfect moments. The mentor who steps up to the plate and dramatically demonstrates humility and authenticity is the mentor who nurtures trust. Luther not only loaned me The Car, he also leveled with me about his errors, struggles, and challenges. The more I saw of his humility, the more I trusted him.

At a large social event in Ovens Auditorium in Charlotte, North Carolina, organized to formally announce his candidacy for the U.S. Senate, Luther was relying openly and heavily on note cards as he began his prepared speech. The audience listened politely. Luther was never very comfortable as a public speaker. Halfway through, he lost his place. He cracked an awkward, apologetic joke and ad-libbed for a moment as he struggled to put his cards in order. Before he could fully recover, the audience broke into supportive applause. It was the sincere, genuine, flawed Luther they adored, not the Luther reading his speech perfectly from notes.

Mask removal is the humble stuff of which trust is made. Humility does not require you to fall on your sword. Nor does it mean loudly advertising your warts and clay feet. It does mean working very hard to be open and vulnerable with protégés. It means remaining alert for opportunities to show empathy (I understand how you feel) rather than sympathy (I feel sad about how you feel). It means working to strip any nuance of rank, power, or status from the relationship. Mentoring is about equality.

CAREFULLY COMMUNICATE COMPETENCE

The mentor's challenge in communicating competence is in not displaying arrogance at the same time. How do you show smartness without being a smart aleck? And there is the flip side: While humility is always a virtue, too much can threaten the protégé's confidence in you. Self-effacing comments, a symbol of modesty if used in moderation, can erode faith if carried too far. "Great leaders," said Luther Hodges to one of my advanced leadership classes, "are willing to let followers see their weak sides. And they are willing to let followers see their strong sides." Call it wholeness, balance, congruence — the goal is a presence that engenders trust.

Therefore, let the protégé hear your pride in your ability. Don't boast; simply acknowledge your good fortune. Be quick to credit others where credit is due: 'I was really lucky to get to understudy Tom Connellan. One of the things Tom taught me was. . . .' Indicate your eagerness to share whatever competence you possess with the protégé. Let the protégé know that although you hold something of superior value, you do not believe that makes you superior.

Putting the 'us' in 'trust' involves remembering that trust occurs in an intimate, interpersonal dimension. Trust is something that happens within people only when it is created between people. Trust is not something that happens by accident; trust is crafted on purpose, with the mentor's full awareness of how his or her actions affect the protégé.

And where does this leave us with Luther and The Car? Luther lost his primary bid for the Senate seat but went on to become undersecretary of commerce in the Carter administration, then chairman of the board of a Washington, D.C., bank. Today he manages a variety of entrepreneurial ventures all over the world from his Phoenix office. He kept The Car for many years, finally selling it in D.C. After thirty years, we still correspond. And there are very few people in the world I trust more than Chairman Hodges.

CHAPTER 7
Scared Students

WHEN FEAR AND LEARNING COLLIDE

Fear has a long and checkered career as an educational tool. Ask a high school counselor and an army drill sergeant about the role of fear in learning and you will get two entirely different answers. In the movie *Stand and Deliver*, Edward James Olmos demonstrates a mentoring style completely at odds with John Houseman's in *The Paper Chase*. (Both films were based on real people. Houseman played Professor Kingsfield, a fictional character based on a real law-school professor. Olmos portrayed Jaime Escalante, a true-life hero of education in Los Angeles.) Some say fear is a healthy partner with learning where simple motor skills are involved — boot camps, skydiving schools, police academies. However, most law students would not say their intimidating law-school experience involved learning a subject that was simple or motor. The debate continues.

This chapter is built on the premise that fear is far more a liability than an asset where learning is involved. A testing, contentious learning environment may bring out the adrenaline but does not bolster aptitude. Learners who are fearful tend to take fewer risks. A work environment that is continually evaluative may discourage growth by minimizing the trial-and-error behavior needed for effective learning.

Nevertheless, some work settings deliberately and consciously infuse evaluation into the setting. A major accounting firm cultivates an up-or-out philosophy, pushing young professionals to make partner by their late thirties or stand ready to be 'made available to the industry.' A certain well-known computer software company demonstrates a low tolerance for error by telling new recruits, 'The cream rises to the top,' 'If you can't stand the heat, get out of the kitchen,' or 'At Bitbucket, Inc., only the strong survive.' Likewise, one large manufacturing company anchors its inspection style on a 'Do it right the first time' philosophy. Since the mentor may have little or no control over an evaluative work environment, how does mentoring work best when the protégé is scared?

The factors in fear reduction are cut from the same philosophical cloth as establishing rapport. However, the approach is different in that 'establish' is replaced with 'overcome' as the goal. While the focus in creating rapport is one of support and openness, the focus in overcoming fear is on strength and compassion. The emphasis is more on weaning than on welcoming.

IRRATIONAL FEELINGS ARE LEGITIMATE FEELINGS

My father passed away in late 1995 at eighty-four, having suffered for his last few years from dementia — an Alzheimer's-like condition that caused his once-sharp mind slowly to deteriorate. Needless to say, to watch this former teacher-coach-banker-farmer go from super intelligent to sadly incoherent was a painful experience for the entire family. Five weeks before he died, my wife, Nancy, and I visited him. His encounter with her gave me new insight into communicating in the midst of fear.

One evening Nancy sat beside him and began to talk with him as if he were normal. He responded by pointing in the air and saying, "There! They're coming to take my land!" She pointed to the same spot and asked, "Are they there?" "Yes," he replied, "and they're mad at me!" She again focused her attention on the imaginary villains and quietly asked, "Might they be coming to visit you because they're worried about you?" There was silence for two or three minutes; then my father smiled and said, "I think you might be onto something." His fear waning, he moved to a new level of mental awareness, and for a time he conversed with her almost as he had years earlier.

Granted, there *are* rational fears. In a foxhole, the fear of being killed is rational. In a fire, the fear of getting burned is rational. At the dentist, the fear of discomfort or pain is rational. There are also rational going-to-work fears. Most fears, however, are not logical — they are psychological. That means they are as imaginary as the villains in the air were to my dad. They are also just as real!

The important contribution the mentor can make in a learning situation is to treat all fears as rational. To say to someone who feels scared, 'You should not feel that way,' is discounting, devaluing, and discourteous. Recall the adage, 'It's easier to turn a mule if you first get him moving.' To overcome fear, start where the protégé is, accepting that position as legitimate. My wife started where my dad was — and from there was able to work with him to bring him out of the grip of his fear.

FEAR IS A THREATENED NEED

Occasions for physical fear are rare in organizational life. Most employees don't worry about getting cement shoes or letter bombs. Physical violence occurs mostly in the funny pages (see Dagwood's tribulations in "Blondie"). On the contrary, organizational fears are generally psychological. People worry about getting rejected, looking foolish, losing power, appearing incompetent, being unemployed — a wide range of fears short of getting booted through a window by Mr. Dithers.

It is not the role of the mentor to become a shrink and psychoanalyze the protégé. However, to be effective in reducing fear, the mentor needs a clear understanding of the protégé's emotional state. If the stated fear is 'I'm not getting a fair shot at the Terri Fritch position,' the real fear might be 'I'm not being recognized for my hard work.' If you can zero in on the real fear, or answer the stated fear while addressing the real fear, your counsel will be more effective.

Psychological needs or drives are the major energy source for individual actions; fear is a secondary response. Think of it as the flip side of a high-priority psychological need. For purposes of this book, let's assume that everyone you mentor places highest value on one of four needs — achievement, recognition, power, or control.

Getting a finer bead on the protégé's priority need is a fundamental part of effective mentoring. As you observe the protégé's actions, keep in mind these four basic needs (based of the renowned research of David McClelland of Harvard). You will find them revealing. (Before we go any further, it is important to say that humans are far too complex to be boxed into just one of four categories. We all have these needs; we differ in part based on the priority that particular needs play in our lives. My high need for control might not be that big a deal in your life; your high need for achievement might be a low priority for me. Both of us have needs for control and achievement; we differ in the relative importance they have in our scheme of things.)

Need for achievement

People who give achievement a high priority are driven in part by a need to measure up, to do well, to succeed. They value challenge and closure and require freedom to perform. Barriers to opportunity frustrate them. They value performance feedback ('This is very creative work') over personal feedback ('You are a very creative person'). They enjoy the professional respect of others but generally do not waste energy being concerned about what others think of them. Their offices or cubicles tend to be furnished with items that are practical and that assist them in achieving a goal.

Need for recognition

Many people are driven by a need for affirmation, respect, and the adoration of others. They engage in actions that gain them approval. They tend to avoid interpersonal conflict, fearing rejection. They value personal feedback, particularly from people in authority. They enjoy being popular with others and are typically (but not universally) highly social. They often display articles that communicate relationships, such as family or group photos, or items that invite the observer to make an affirming comment.

Need for power

People with power as a high-priority need enjoy dominance over others. They demand respect and loyalty. They can be temperamental and explosive, especially on issues of loyalty or the potential of losing dominance. They can be passive or aggressive bullies, surrounding themselves with people they can dominate. They put energy into symbols of power and status as confirmation to themselves and reminders to others. Whether title, club, car, or corner office, they require signs and symbols of authority.

Need for control

The need to control has behavioral similarities with the need for power. However, the focus is less on domination of people and more on domination of events or situations. Control people tend to be nitpickers, often devoting energy to form over substance. If their control is threatened, they quickly become frustrated, sometimes resorting to fits and pouts. They are generally on top of the details of their operation, even though their need for order might show up as an obsession with neatness.

"Education is the ability to listen to almost anything without losing your temper or your self-confidence."
— Robert Frost

So — what to do with all of this? Several steps can transform your observations into better understanding of your protégé. Pay close attention to her actions and ask: What need might she be fulfilling by selecting this action? Examine moments of anger. Anger, like fear, is a secondary feeling; the root issue is generally a frustrated need. People with a high need for achievement have a fear of failing; people with a high need for recognition have a fear of rejection; people with a high need for power have a fear of appearing weak; and people with a high need for control have a fear of being wrong. Remember: The higher priority the need plays in the protégé's life, the more fearful (and angry) she will be if she perceives a threat to her need.

Look at the possessions the protégé chooses and displays. If you see awards or degrees on the wall, what does that tell you about the person? What about someone who displays pictures of family or friends? What kind of person drives a flashy sports car? Any one of these factors by itself may tell you little. However, an accumulation of observations, the overall pattern of behavior, can give you vital insights into the things that are most important to the protégé.

FEAR IS A MIRROR OF SELF-ESTEEM

Let's assume you now have a clearer understanding of the person. What's next? The first thing you can do is to pay attention to the nuances, the subtle cues, the subtext of your discussions with your protégé — anything that might signal some fear that needs to be addressed. Then, answer the literal words of a question while you address the deeper issue that you think might be fueling the protégé's fear.

You also can play a major role in bolstering the protégé's low self-esteem and thus help to push fear out. Mentors do not give courage, they uncover courage. Two ways you can help the protégé find hidden courage are:

- **Use lots of positive affirmations!** Mentors sometimes approach protégés as though affirmations are rare and expensive gifts to be doled out parsimoniously. Somewhere they heard that too much praise would make a protégé lazy. This is a sad fallacy. William James, the great psychologist-philosopher, said it well: "The deepest craving of humans is the need to be appreciated." Look for things to compliment; lavish praise with sincerity and enthusiasm.

- **Assume that the protégé has no reason for low self-esteem.** This means never buying into a protégé's low opinion of himself. Although this may sound harsh, it can be a powerful gift. This subtle message in the mentor's attitude will become self-fulfilling and in time help the protégé let go of the old self-view and assume a new feeling of worth. Remember *My Fair Lady*? Professor Henry Higgins wanted to see whether he could take a lowly flower girl from the streets of London and train her so well that he could pass her off as a member of the nobility at an upper-crust ball. As Eliza Doolittle learned the ways and speech of an aristocratic lady, she became one.

Fear is a barrier to learning. When protégés bring fear into a learning environment, they limit the depth and breadth of their growth. Great mentors are fear
hunters. Invite your protégé to hunt fear with you, and together enjoy the bounty
of your success.

CHAPTER 8

For the Protégé

CALMING THE ANXIOUS HEART

Mentoring books rarely speak to protégés. And there aren't many books out there about how to be a good protégé. This book is different. Mentoring should be a partnership, an act of reciprocal learning. As such, it is important for both partners to do their part in making their joint exploration an effective one.

This chapter is the first of four about the protégé's part in that process. I have been a protégé many times, some good and some not so good. I have tried to remember what it felt like — what went through my head and heart. I also interviewed a lot of people who were protégés in a formal mentoring relationship. This feature of the book is a compilation of that 'stand in your shoes' effort.

The 'For the Protégé' chapters will have a script-like format. When you read them, you will be in the position of protégé in a story that traces the unfolding of a mentoring relationship. And you will be the only real person in this story. Your mentor is made up. His name is Dale and his character is a mixture of a lot of typical mentors. Dale's role is like a prop — not a central part of this story — to help you explore your thoughts and feelings about the experience of mentoring. You are the main focal point, and so your words are always in bold print.

There is one other made-up character in this four-part story. Appropriately named Sage, she (or he) is that brilliant part of you that is all-knowing and never at a loss for what to do or say. Sage is your tap-on-the-shoulder, whisper-in-the-ear guru who mentors you through your relationship with Dale. Imagine Sage looking any way you want . My Sage looks like that elderly white-bearded elf in the Keebler's® Cookies ad a few years ago, or the way some children's books portray Sneezy in *Snow White and the Seven Dwarfs*, but he is the size of Tinkerbell in *Peter Pan*. Sage's words appear in italics.

Our story opens on a fall morning, the first day of sunshine after a week of overcast skies and rain. You are meeting with Dale for the first time. Dale will also be your project leader on an effort that will take at least six months, maybe a year. When the project is completed Dale will be preparing an assessment of your performance to be included in your personnel file, along with the assessment of others associated with or affected by the project. You know who Dale is, but you don't really know him. Dale's cubicle is tucked away in a hard-to-find corner of the building. The room contains three identical cubicles; Dale's is in the middle.

"Where the heck is this place? I should have brought bread crumbs to find my way back."

"You'll find it, and everything will work out terrific. Walk slower… you have plenty of time! And walk stately… like you own this place. Hold your head up! Good! Now take a couple of really deep breaths."

"Dale's probably not even there. Seems like his cubicle is in the middle of a row of cubicles. I'll bet there will be a bunch of people able to eavesdrop on everything we say. What am I doing here?"

"He WILL be there… remember, he called you twice to confirm the time. And what if there ARE people within earshot? People in the cubicle next to yours listen to you talking with your best friend about some pretty sensitive topics. So lighten up! You'll do great! Think about two things: First, what you want to get out of this experience, not how you'll do. Second, think about how you can help Dale best deliver a really great mentoring performance."

"Okay, okay. My goal for this experience: to get through it alive!"

You find yourself getting tickled at your own humor. It occurs to you there are similarities to joking at a time like this and whistling in the dark when you walked home from a friend's house when you were a kid. You wind through a few twists and turns. Then you spot the row of cubicles Dale had described in his directions when the two of you last spoke. Dale is standing in the entrance with a big grin. You discover your fear is giving way to the front edge of excitement.

"You must be Dale," you find yourself saying. **"I'm glad you could see me today."**

Dale directs you to a seat and offers to get you a cup of coffee. You say thanks as you sit down and take a pass on the coffee.

"Great job… you're starting off on the right foot. Let Dale have the floor and guide you through how the conversation is to unfold. Remember, help Dale deliver greatness! When the time comes, you can tell Dale clearly your goals for this experience."

As if right on cue, Dale starts the conversation on goals. Your turn comes when he asks about yours.

"Yes, Dale, I do have a few goals. I'm new to the process we will be using on project documentation, and I know you've had a lot of experience. I also want to learn more about how to deal with multiple clients who have conflicting demands on my time. Too often, I get caught in the middle. If I satisfy one client I disappoint the other. Sometimes I avoid them both since I know it will be a no-win situation."

"Remember the other part ... YOU have a responsibility to Dale. Now, go ahead and talk about it!"

"Oh, and Dale ... there is one other goal I have for this experience. I want to do everything I can to make this a great mentoring experience for you."

Dale looks surprised and noticeably pleased. He responds awkwardly but is obviously moved. You suddenly sense this relationship just got bumped up to a higher level.

"You're doing a great job. This is going to work out! Don't you think?"

Part III

Accepting:
CREATING A SAVE HAVEN FOR RISK TAKING

Accepting

CREATING A SAFE HAVEN FOR RISK TAKING

Pope John XXIII was probably the most beloved pope of this century. The devotion people felt for him was due in part to the fact that he was completely without pretense. His openness and humility endeared him to millions, Catholic and non-Catholic alike. One of his first official acts was to visit the prisoners in a large penal institution in Rome. As he gave the inmates his blessing, he shared with them the fact that he had been in a prison, too — to visit his cousin!

Sidney Jourard, in his classic *The Transparent Self*, describes countless research studies demonstrating conclusively that humans have a natural, built-in tendency to be open and revealing. When that tendency is thwarted, the individual reacts by becoming closed, cautious, and reserved. The longer this blockage occurs, the more difficult it is for trusting relationships to develop. In his book *Why Am I Afraid to Tell You Who I Am?*, John Powell answers his title question, "Because if I tell you who I am, you may not like who I am, and it's all that I have."

In the last few chapters we explored different dimensions of the core competency and first step in the mentoring process: *surrendering*. In Part III we will examine the second crucial core competency of great mentoring: accepting. Accepting is evaluation-free, egalitarian encountering — mentoring without arrogance, bias, prejudice, or selectivity.

Accepting means inviting the learner to be courageous, to take the risks needed to unfreeze old habits and to embrace and internalize new practices. This entails sending all manner of signals and signs that hearten the learner to boldness and provide support, despite unstable first attempts and timid trials. The mentor's willingness to act in ways that are noticeably gallant is a part of that invitational signaling process. Such actions say to the protégé, 'I value you enough to accept you despite your imperfections.' Think of it as a human form of grace. (Grace among some religious groups means 'undeserved forgiveness.')

Mentors who are effective at demonstrating acceptance also foster a spirit of inquiry on a level emotional playing field — a relationship with unrestricted access, from which all issues unrelated to learning are barred. They reveal a riveting curiosity in the protégé through their dramatic listening, empathetic inquiry, and productive dialogue. When mentors listen to learn (not to instruct), when mentors question to unearth (not to prove), and when mentors converse to explore (not to boast or best), the protégé experiences acceptance.

The next five chapters focus on skills and techniques that support competence in accepting. This part begins with the most crucial accepting skill — encouraging courage — and ends with a glimpse into what accepting looks like from the protégé's side of the equation.

CHAPTER 9
Invitations to Risk
ACCEPTANCE AS A NURTURER OF COURAGE

Learning can be a scary proposition. The protégé's path is not only potentially embarrassing, awkward, and unpleasant, it generally comes with no guarantee of success. And learning in its most raw form almost always entails a public display of weakness. Learning without entry into the discomfort zone is not likely to be true learning. Learning without facing some chance of failure is superficial progress, not real change.

Learners are brave pioneers. They leave a comfortable, safe 'who I am' in search of an unknown, vulnerable 'who I can be.' They are willing to withstand emotional 'arrows in the back' as they blaze unfamiliar territory, abandoning a space of inner security to engage in temporary recklessness. They boldly take steps knowing skinned knees (and egos) are in the offing. There is a sort of an emotional masochism at play when an imagined benefit outweighs established certainty and the learner deliberately plunges into a realm of probable anxiety. What can a mentor do to support that pioneering recklessness? What can a mentor do to stir learner bravery?

Courage is not an attribute or quality to be bestowed, despite our language to the contrary. We don't really *give* courage, as if it is something one imparts or donates to another. Instead, think of courage as a preexisting condition, there to be awakened. Like a shy child on the fringe of a noisy party, courage is a trait that is already present but in need of an invitation to 'join the fun.' The role of mentor is to partner with the protégé to surface courage and then to support the protégé in recognizing its presence. Acceptance is the context in which that surfacing and supporting occurs.

Acceptance entails actions that communicate unconditional positive regard. Acceptance is confirmation without concurrence. It says, 'I value you even if I disagree with you or disapprove of your actions.' Acceptance is a living announcement of worth. In a mentoring partnership, it is an invitation to risk, extended to the protégé in three ways: dynamic modeling, judgment-free communication, and rational affirmation.

INVITATION ONE: DYNAMIC MODELING

"Leaders are much more powerful role models when they learn than when they teach," says Harvard professor Rosabeth Moss Kanter. There is no more effective teaching technique than personal example. If you are inviting the protégé to take risks and you also engage in risk taking, you are communicating acceptance. Courage hidden will join courage displayed. Remember our analogy of courage being like a shy child at a party? A public request by the host of the party for all shy children to join in the fun is not likely to invoke participation. But if another child makes a private, personal but determined invitation, the outcome will be completely different.

The modeling of courage needs to be dynamic, not subtle. Dynamic modeling means you act as an obvious prototype for the protégé. Courage building requires far more than cheerleading support from the sidelines. And this is no time to try to let nuance and nicety carry the day. Dynamic modeling requires 'Follow me!' behavior that is obvious and noticeable. Why? A protégé's reluctance to be bold is sometimes fueled by the absence of a 'show how it's done' example.

'I read this great article on . . . ,' 'I met with Sue because I knew she could teach me how to . . . ,' and 'The course I'm taking on the Internet has helped me to. . . .' — all are examples of dynamic modeling that telegraph two things: an allegiance to continuous learning and an enthusiastic participation in the process. Your goal is not to model being a fan of learning. Your goal is to model being a learner — and a passionate one! Help your learning actions get up on a table and shout!

> "Honesty is the cornerstone of all success, without which confidence and ability to perform shall cease to exist."
> — Mary Kay Ash

Take your protégé to a seminar, conference, workshop -- anywhere you can learn together. Ask your protégé to teach you something she or he knows that you'd like to learn. If you attend a conference or seminar, make time to share with your protégé the highlights of your learning and what you plan to do with your newfound knowledge. If your protégé attends a seminar, class, or conference, schedule time to pick his or her brain afterwards. Celebrate people who boldly pursue growth — the clerk who finishes a degree after several years' interlude, the supervisor who tutors after hours, or the operator who writes an article for a local trade magazine.

End meetings by soliciting suggestions for improvement on how to make the next meeting better. Invite unique people to attend — people who offer a point of view or perspective that can challenge, provoke, and inspire. Keep a 'sages on call' list — inventors, artists, writers, anyone who can provide new ways of seeing challenges, attacking problems, or inventing solutions.

INVITATION TWO:
JUDGMENT-FREE COMMUNICATION

Anatomy experts tell us that courage occurs physiologically when the circuits in the thinking portion of the brain — the cerebral cortex — turn on and restrain or curb the over-excited emotional center of the brain. This means that rather than being emotionally stymied, clear thinking directs action even in the face of risks. Mentors see the opportunities for collective exploration as chances to make good even better. Focusing on their role as the conveyor of wisdom, mentors have a confident view and see no minefields of emotional loss. However, protégés enter collective exploration looking up at a setting filled with the possibility for failure. In their mind's eye they witness extremely foolish comments and grossly disappointing faux pas. They believe that somehow their hidden inadequacies — ones they view as massive — will suddenly be exposed and come under the disapproving scrutiny of a critical judge. Weighed by this exaggerated perception of reality, hearts race, memories halt, and the entire speaking apparatus is abruptly inoperative . . . and bone dry!

This is where nonjudgmental communication works as a magical antidote. Instead of a tone of censure, great mentors communicate the warmth of acceptance. An open posture replaces the cross-armed stare a protégé might anticipate. Their pace is slow and deliberate, not clipped and ambiguous. Gestures are invitational and affirming, not negative and tentative. Nonjudgmental communication uses nonthreatening expressions such as 'What were your reasons for . . . ?' instead of 'Why did you . . . ?' Great mentors' facial expressions are more like you would see on people watching an entertaining nature film than observing a losing ballgame.

Above all, nonjudgmental communication works by sending a friendly message that the protégé's emotional armor is unnecessary and can be discarded. The key is to make the message an act of discovery — based on the idea that the protégé's view is completely legitimate and normal, but also inaccurate. This is best done by refraining from commenting on the protégé's nervousness directly. Instead, talk with the protégé as if anxiety were nowhere in sight. It is also important to use some self-effacing 'I'm just like you' comments or examples. Mentor vulnerability is a powerful tool in dissipating protégé fear.

INVITATION THREE:
RATIONAL AFFIRMATION

Ever thought about the role of cheering at an athletic event? We don't watch in silence. But neither are our shouts of pleasure when our favorite team is winning like the sounds we might make if we sank a hole in one or won the sweepstakes. Cheering is not simply an expression of joy, but also one of affirmation. Our intent is to encourage, support, and coax. When sports announcers speak of the 'home field advantage,' they are acknowledging the power of affirmation as a tool for summoning courage.

'Rational affirmation' is an intentional oxymoron. Remember, evoking courage is about quieting the overactive, irrational anxiety in the protégé. Flattering the protégé with some schmaltzy, generalized 'Attaboy!' will surely be considered patronizing . . . the protégé is likely to be thinking, 'You clearly see my foibles and are just trying to be nice to me.' The goal is to communicate in a form that is accurate and clear (like the football versions of 'Go defense!') yet sunny in its nature. Affirmations should be straightforward ('You ask very good questions that make me see things in a new way') and never contrived or backhanded ('For a fat lady you sure don't sweat much!'—that's the punch line from an old corny joke!).

An effective mentor invites the protégé to face the risks of learning by being a good model, engaging in judgment-free communication, and offering rational (i.e., believable) affirmation. When the protégé witnesses courage, hears the sound of courage, and feels the glow of courage, experimentation ensues and wisdom results.

Mr. Kirkland was my biology teacher in the tenth grade. When the topic of the birds and the bees surfaced on the school curriculum, it was greeted by a wealth of snickers and a scarcity of questions. In the late fifties, there was no one more awkward than a sixteen-year-old boy in a mixed-gender class when the topic of classroom discussion was human anatomy and sex education. But, Mr. Kirkland had a solution. Realizing the boys needed some special coaxing, he met with all of us boys after school.

He talked openly of his own awkwardness and curiosity about anatomy and sex when he was a young boy. He was completely nonjudgmental in tone. Then he invited our candid questions. When the first brave soul risked a question, Mr. Kirkland was quick with affirmation and support. Before long we had a lively discussion underway about topics that were formerly only whispered privately among super close friends. The after school discussion gave all of us the courage to take the biology class more seriously and to provide assertive leadership in the regular classroom discussions. Great mentors summon learner courage with the enticement of sincere acceptance.

CHAPTER 10
Socrates' Greatest Secret
AWESOME QUERIES

If there were a Mentors' Hall of Fame, Socrates would be an instant inductee. In a heated argument over whether slaves have souls (the ancient Greeks believed that only smart people would have eternal life), Socrates bet a case of mead (Greek for Bud Light®) that he could teach a common slave the Pythagorean theorem (for those who used it in high school and then filed it away: the square of the hypotenuse of a right triangle is equal to the sum of the squares of the other two sides). He had no overhead projector, handouts, or textbook. He needed only two tools to teach the slave: the capacity to ask the right question and the ability to listen carefully to the meaning behind the answer. To this day the method behind his bold bet is memorialized as Socratic teaching.

Socrates understood the secret of mentoring: Effective questioning brings insight, which fuels curiosity, which cultivates wisdom. Now we will examine, methodically and anecdotally, how the Socratic method works. You will learn why Socrates' secret is such a powerful one.

I have a friend who returned from a family reunion in a tiny town in rural South Carolina. He is a prominent surgeon at a major hospital and teaches part time at a prestigious medical school. "I finally realized," he told me, "why I remember my childhood as a painfully boring experi-

> "It's an unanswered question, but let us still believe in the dignity and importance of the question."
> — Tennessee Williams

ence." He took off his reading glasses and momentarily stared into space. "There was no growth, and I was frightened that I might be trapped in a tomb of intellectual stagnation."

At first I thought his assessment seemed too bitter and his reaction arrogant. He went on to describe his early days of living in an imaginary world for weeks at a time just to avoid the monotony of a small-town life in which change was shunned and uniqueness punished. He hid in books because conversations with others offered only shallow and perfunctory mental activity. He talked to his pets, which understood him but couldn't talk back.

His withdrawal into himself opened the way to academic achievement, escape from stagnation, and eventual success. For many years he blamed the pain of his youth on the misfortune of growing up in a boring setting. However, his return to his childhood home gave him new insight. It was not the unstimulating environment but rather the dearth of curiosity that had imprisoned his soul.

"They have great barbecue," he remarked with a smile, describing the weekend reunion, "But they don't ask questions." I prodded him to explain. "People at the reunion talked; there was a lot of conversation. And there was a lot of concerned communication. But no one really interviewed me. Oh, I got quite a few fact-finding questions, but no follow-ups. No one was really curious about my life — only concerned about being polite. I even tried to seed the encounters by working hard to learn about their views, feelings, ideas, joys, and fears. They seemed eager to give me a peek into their souls. But after such a one-sided dialogue, I left South Carolina feeling highly informed about their world, but lonely and bored."

His sad story made me reflect on the role that questions — real questions, the search for understanding — can play in growth. Quality questions have a multiplier effect on learning. Ask an information-seeking question, you get only an answer or a fact; ask an understanding-seeking question and you unleash a more powerful chain of events. Here's how it works.

THE CREATIVE HUMAN COMPUTER

The human brain is often compared with a computer, but it is actually very different. Most computers are largely information-storage devices. Ask an information-seeking question, and the computer goes into a retrieval mode — as does the human brain. However, ask an understanding-seeking question, and the mind has to make up an answer not found in the storage closet of the brain. Computers cannot make up answers. Understanding-seeking questions stimulate the kind of mental activity that creates insight or discovery. As the mind leaps and turns and twists to respond to an understanding-seeking question, special new synapses are activated and the insight experience occurs.

"Insight is the brain at play," brain researcher Pierce Howard, author of *The Owner's Manual for the Brain*, told me recently, "and the brain loves to play." Discovery — that 'Aha!' experience of finding a connection, closing a gap, completing a pattern — is very rewarding to the mind. So rewarding, in fact, that the mind is constantly on the lookout for an opportunity to repeat the experience. And the more 'Aha's!' the mind gets, the hungrier the mind is for them. Finding information is easy and boring; crafting understanding is challenging and exhilarating. The more the mind experiences creative discovery, the more the mind hunts another insight. This pursuit of insight or discovery is what we call 'curiosity.' To the mind, curiosity is its own reward. And the by-product of perpetual curiosity is wisdom.

HOW TO ASK QUESTIONS

How does the mentor start this insight-curiosity-wisdom chain? One major chain starter is the understanding-seeking question. Great mentors, aware that their objective is to foster wisdom, are skilled at asking these questions. Below are several important techniques for crafting and asking questions that produce insight.

Start with a Setup Statement

This may seem strange, but the best way to ask an insight-producing question is to start with a statement. Here's the reason: Questions can be more powerful if the sender and receiver are clearly on the same wavelength — and know that they are. Starting with a setup statement establishes identification and context. It creates a milieu that makes the follow-up question much more powerful.

> Mentor: (Setup) Jan, you've been working for about eight weeks now on the Dunn review.

> Protégé: (Answer) That's right. I've had to put in some long hours on it.

> Mentor: (Question) What have you learned about the project that you didn't expect to learn?

Notice how much more effective the question is after the mentor first makes a statement to establish identification (I am on your wavelength) and context (We have now established what area we are focusing on). It communicates to the protégé, 'I've done my homework, I care, I'm eager to learn with you.' It also helps the protégé to focus cleanly on the question and not on establishing a background to shore up the answer. Imagine how defensive the question alone might make the protégé feel.

Ask Questions That Require Higher-Level Thinking

Remember that the ultimate goal is to create insight, not to share information. Granted, some information sharing may be necessary; the main objective, however, is to nurture understanding and growth, not just exchange facts. Construct questions that require the protégé to dig deep to answer. Questions that force comparisons can accomplish this: 'What are ways the Hollar project was different from the Dickinson Project?' Questions that require synthesis can induce deeper thinking: 'What do you see as the key implications of Mr. Rivers' assessment?' And questions that call for evaluation can provoke higher-level thinking: 'If you could handle that assignment again, what would you do differently?'

The conventional wisdom on questioning has always been to ask open-ended questions. Closed questions, the lesson goes, will cause the receiver to deliver a short, single-word or -phrase answer. However, the process is more complex than that. Socrates' understanding-seeking questions did not just make the slave talk — they made him think. Anyone with a teenager knows that the answers to questions beginning with 'what,' 'how,' and 'why' can be as short as those for a yes-no question. The intent of questioning to seek understanding is not just more words in the answer, but more depth in the thinking needed to produce the answer.

Avoid Questions That Begin with Why

Why avoid 'why' questions? The point was made earlier, but it bears repeating. In most cultures, a sentence that begins with the word 'why' and ends in a question mark is usually perceived as judgmental and indicting. Granted, body language can play a role in how such questions are perceived, but even with perfect body language, our antennae go up as soon as we hear a 'why' question.

Find ways to soften the interrogatory question. 'Why did you do that?' can sound very different from 'What were your reasons for doing that?' The word 'why' is not the problem; it is putting 'why' on the front of a question. As we learned earlier, judgment can turn an open atmosphere into one of protection, caution, and guarded behavior. Without vulnerability there is no risk; without risk there is no experimentation and growth.

Use Curiosity To Stimulate Curiosity

Socrates did more than ask good questions. Socrates demonstrated an enthusiasm for the learning process. He believed in it and was excited to participate in demonstrating it. Attitude is as much a part of the Socratic method as technique.

A few years ago stereographic pictures became the rage. People stared at them for long periods, trying to find the image or object among what seemed a random mixture of colored dots. I watched a teenage girl in a shopping mall help her boyfriend 'see' a picture she had earlier figured out. The girl and boy were equally curious, both eager for the image to be discovered again, both excited when the insight finally came to him. Mentoring is like that.

Great mentors are not only curious; they are excited by the opportunity to stimulate other people's curiosity. Their attitude is 'I can't wait to see the lights come on for you!' They are open about their excitement and verbally communicate pleasure when the protégé's 'Aha!' finally comes.

Take stock of the greatest mentors down through the ages — Jesus, Buddha, Moses, Mohammed, Confucius, Lao-tse, to name a few. Their influence was due in part to their ability to challenge their learners with thought-provoking questions. The same is true of modern mentors. In a study done a few years ago, Fortune 500 CEOs were asked what contributed most to their success. Many listed an effective mentor as one of the key factors. To the question of what made these important people so influential, the most common response harked back to mead and Socrates: They asked great questions. Questions are the jewels of mentoring.

Assessing Your Inquiry Talents

The Mentor Scale can be a helpful tool in examining your talents and blind spots with regard to inquiry. Below are a few things to watch out for, tied to the scoring form you completed in chapter 3.

Sociability

LOW: Watch out for too much silence. If the protégé does not answer in ten seconds, she may need for you to redirect the question. Also, know that eye contact can be important in conveying a sincere interest in the protégé's answers. Tape your conversations to self-evaluate your style of inquiry.

HIGH: Beware of not giving the protégé an opportunity to answer. Silence can be golden. Pause after asking a question. If you are susceptible to this trap, count to ten after asking a question and before asking another or rephrasing the one you just asked. Assume that the protégé heard and understood and is simply contemplating an answer.

Dominance

LOW: Think before you ask. You may tend to let the interaction wander by asking questions just to ask questions. Consider your goal and focus. Determine what you seek to learn, then choose questions that will take you there.

HIGH: You may have a tendency to craft questions that give you the answer you like to hear. Leading the protégé is just as inappropriate and ineffective as leading the witness. Soften your tone; make sure your approach does not make the protégé feel as though he were on trial.

Openness

LOW: Avoid keeping your questions too much on the surface. While invading privacy is not the goal, your aim is to foster in-depth thinking. Be willing to allow a bit of controversy; conflict is nothing more than a symptom of tension. When you accurately interpret and work through conflict by your candor and openness, interpersonal closeness and valuable creativity will be the likely byproduct.

HIGH: You may often find yourself wanting to answer for the protégé. Back off and give the person a chance to communicate her thoughts. It is also important to avoiding getting too personal too quickly. While you may be more than ready to foster closeness, the protégé may need a bit more time.

■

"He holds him with his glittering eye —
    The wedding guest stood still,
And listens like a three year's child:
    The Mariner hath his will."
— Samuel Taylor Coleridge,
    The Rime of the Ancient Mariner

CHAPTER 11
The Ear of an Ally
THE LOST ART OF LISTENING

I 'll bet there are not more than two supervisors on earth who do not sense the importance of being a good listener! It matters not whether the person has ever attended a leadership class, read an article on supervision, or studied a manager who is a good listener. If you've never heard of the importance of listening, you're a card-carrying alien from some other galaxy!

Knowing that listening is important and *being* a good listener are two very different things. Ask employees about the listening skills of their bosses, and most will give them at best a C+. With zillions of books on how leaders should listen, why do employees continue to ding their bosses on listening? Is this a competence crisis?

In my experience, the gap between 'should' and 'would' has less to do with communication management than with noise management. Most leaders *can* be great listeners. Let their eight-year-old come home crying about a neighborhood conflict and you will see great listening. Zero in on a quiet corner conversation in the funeral home during the wake for a friend and you will see great listening. Put a leader between a hostile union steward and a potential shut-you-down strike and you will witness some of the best listening in history. Yet, mix the normal pace of work, the typical persona of 'I'm the boss,' and the traditional orientation that 'employees don't need to be babied,' and you have the prescription for 'just get to the punch line' leader listening.

Listening is crucial to mentoring. Ask fifty people who had great mentors what attribute they found most crucial, and forty-nine will probably mention their mentors' listening: 'I felt I had his undivided attention when I most needed it.' 'You felt there was absolutely nothing happening on the face of the globe but you, her, and your problem.' 'He was so engaged in my concern that his secretary had to interrupt us to tell him his phone had been ringing. I sure wasn't going to mention it.'

How do the best mentors evade the demands of daily distractions to give dedicated listening? The sounds of great listening tell us effective listeners don't *start* doing anything special — they *stop* doing something normal.

FOCUS ON FOCUS

Great mentors get focused and stay focused. When listening is their goal, they make it the priority. They do not let *anything* distract. A wise leader once said, 'There are no individuals at work more important to your success than your employees — not your boss, not your customers, not your vendors. When an employee needs you to listen, pretend you just got a gift of five minutes with your greatest hero. For me, it's Abraham Lincoln.' What a great concept! Think about it. If you could have five minutes — and *only* five minutes — with Moses, Mozart, or Mother Teresa, would you let a call from your boss, your customer, or anyone eat up part of that precious time? Treat your employees with the same focus and priority.

'Hold my calls,' 'Let's get out of here so we can really talk,' or 'Tell him I'll have to call back' are words that telegraph noise management. They say to employees, 'What you have to say is so important that I don't want to miss a single word.' If you cannot give employees the 'I've got five minutes with Bill Gates, George Bush, or Billy Graham' kind of focus, postpone the encounter until you can. It's better to say, 'Jill, I want to give you my undivided attention. But I'm two hours from a crucial meeting and, to be perfectly honest, I would be giving you only half my attention. Can we schedule this later today when I can really focus?'"

Assume the Reporter Position

Try this the next time you need to listen to someone: Imagine that you're a newspaper reporter from another culture sent here on assignment to get the story and report it. Your readers cannot see, hear, or feel this story except through your words. They also know nothing about the culture; you must rely on every tiny clue, nuance, and symbol to get the story right.

Your first interviewee is sitting before you, talking. It is your protégé. Now in your role as a foreign reporter, describe every subtlety in the protégé's tone, gesture, or expression. Notice especially the eyes — what have been called the 'windows to the soul.' Pretend you do not know this person and are hearing her speak to you for the first time. Listen for her choice of words and expressions. Is there a deeper meaning behind the sentences you hear? Is there a message that is not initially obvious in the communication?

If you ask a question or make a statement, how quick is the protégé's response? What might be implied by her silence? Is her laughter polite, muted, or hearty? If her words and tone could be a song, what style of music would it be — a country song, a rap tune, a chorale, a gospel hymn? If a great painter were to use this person's words as the inspiration for a picture, what might appear on the canvas? What color is the protégé's tone or mood?

Listening, done well, is complete absorption. Ever watch Larry King on CNN? His success as an interviewer lies not in his questions but in his terrific listening skills. He zips right past the interviewee's words, sentences, and paragraphs to get to the meaning. The mission of listening is to be so tuned into the other person's message that understanding becomes a copy-and-paste function from one mind to another. Perhaps the expression 'meeting of the minds' should be changed to 'joining of the minds.' Dramatic listening is not just a rendezvous of brains; it is a uniting, a linkage, a partnership. Like all human connections, it requires constant effort and commitment.

BE A MIRROR, NOT A MEMORY

One of my biggest challenges in striving to be a good parent was simply to listen without an agenda. Whenever my son began to catalog his concerns, convictions, or curiosity, I would usually feel the need to make a point, teach a lesson, correct an action, or offer some caution. When I finally gave up trying to be a smart daddy and worked at being simply a mirror, he began to open up, trust, and — most important — feel heard.

When he asked, "How would you . . . ?" I would work hard to remember to ask what he would do — before I offered an opinion. When he voiced frustration or concern, before I answered I tried first to communicate through my actions that his message had gotten through — especially when my answer was likely to be different from the one he thought he was going to get. The adage 'You are not eligible to change my view until you first show that you understand my view' serves you in two ways. First, it helps you stay focused on being heard rather than making points. Second, it tells your listener that he is important.

PUT YOUR PROTÉGÉ IN CHARGE OF CUEING YOU

Being a poor listener is habit forming. Focusing takes effort; mirroring takes patience. Meanwhile, the clock is ticking on getting that order out, the boss wants to know where's the Blaha report you promised to have done yesterday, two calls are on hold, three people are pacing the waiting room, and you're finishing up a meeting with your protégé. Who could be a great listener under these circumstances? Answer: not even Superman! You need assistance from the only person who can help you — your protégé!

Here's how you ask for it: 'George, I need your help. I know there are times when I'm not the listener I want to be. But most of the time when I'm being a lousy listener, I'm not aware I'm doing it. That's where you can help. When you think you're not getting my undivided attention, I'd appreciate your letting me know. I may get better, I may reschedule our meeting to a better time, or I may just keep on being a lousy listener. But I don't have a shot at improving unless I know when I need to, and you're the best person to tell me.'

Protégés are not stupid. They will hear the words of your request, but they'll be skeptical until they see you act. You may have to ask several times before your protégé takes you at your word. And unless you express your gratitude — no matter how accurate the assessment or how successful the result — your protégé may decide not to risk your displeasure, and withdraw. Prime the feedback pump, conscientiously listen to and value whatever you get, and, in time, the quality and helpfulness of the feedback will improve.

Good mentors do not listen passively; they listen dramatically. They demonstrate through their words and actions that the thoughts of their protégés are welcome and useful. When people feel heard, they feel valued. Feeling valued, they are more likely to take risks and experiment. Only through trying new steps do they grow and learn. The bottom line is this: If your goal is to be a great mentor, start by using your noise-management skills to help you fully use your talents as a great listener.

CHAPTER 12
'Give and Take' starts with 'Give'

DISTINGUISHED DIALOGUES

Dialogue is defined as an "interchange of ideas, especially when open and frank, as in seeking mutual understanding or harmony." Effective dialogue — with emphasis on 'di' (meaning two) — requires a level playing field, equality, and give-and-take. These dynamics raise dialogue from a simple question-and-answer session to a rich, creative interaction that is more than the sum of its parts.

Recall the conversations you have most valued in your life. What elements made the dialogue positive and productive? You can probably identify several. First, each player valued the view of the other, even if the views were different. The give-and-take was one in which both parties could give undivided attention and keep the dialogue focused. Finally, the outcome was that learning occurred, issues were resolved, or understanding was reached. These three components — valuing, give-and-take, and closure — will form the basis of our look at dialogue in the mentoring relationship.

THE MAGIC OF MIND-SET

There is a moment in the Edward Albee play *Who's Afraid of Virginia Woolf?* in which George and Martha (played in the film version by Richard Burton and Elizabeth Taylor) stop their perpetual oral battle to discover that they have been arguing over completely different subjects. The same thing often happens, at various decibel levels, in our own conversations. 'What were we talking about?' 'I forgot what I was saying,' and 'Where were we?' tell us that we're involved in off-track, out-of-sync, or unrelated conversations.

'Mind-set' is the term for the tone-setting actions at the beginning of a discussion that ensure a meeting of the minds on three simple but powerful questions. If both mentor and protégé are of one mind on these questions, the discussion will probably have a positive outcome.

- Why are we here? Both parties need to be clear on the purpose of the conversation. A simple statement followed by confirmation is usually enough: 'Rachel, I see this session as an opportunity for the two of us to discuss the best approach for conducting the Boyd study. Is that your goal as well?'

- What will it mean to you? The potential for both participants to benefit from the dialogue is important. Not only does it help focus the exchange, it enhances motivation. Proper attention to the potential benefits for the protégé can turn a lethargic, 'Here we go again, another meeting with Gilbert' mind-set into 'Wow, this meeting with Gilbert is going to be really helpful!' The mentor derives the satisfaction of helping the protégé learn to the benefit of all.

- How shall we talk? Mind-set also includes telegraphing the tone and style needed. Even if the tone is implied, a brief reminder can be useful in serving notice that an open, candid, freewheeling conversation is needed and expected. It also helps clarify the rules of engagement, avoiding unpleasant surprises: 'Mary Nell, I'll be as open and candid as I can in this discussion. My thought was that we devote about thirty minutes to exploring options, then give you a chance to make a decision.'

PRIMING THE PUMP

The expression 'priming the pump' had real meaning when I was a child. In the backyard of my grandfather's home was a water pump that required priming to function. You 'seeded' water from the ground by pouring a large pitcher of water into the top and then pumping madly up and down on the handle. To a young boy who thought that water came from a faucet, 'water making' — wringing water out of the earth by your own efforts — had special magic.

If there is ever a time when the word 'catalyst' applies to the role of mentor, it is during dialogue. The human version of priming the pump is assisting insight making by helping the discussion accomplish its function. There are five skills associated with catalyzing the give-and-take of dialogue: asking initiating or clarifying questions, paraphrasing, summarizing, extending, and using nonverbal cues.

Ask Initiating or Clarifying Questions

An earlier chapter on Socrates' secret (chapter 10) explored the art of stimulating learning by asking questions. The questions that work best are those that are direct but not leading — especially open-ended questions, those beginning with what, when, where, or how. Here are some examples of open-ended questions helpful in initiating and clarifying:

'What was the most challenging part of the task?'

'How did your team approach the problem?'

'Describe what makes this technique important.'

'What are your remaining questions?'

'What have I not asked that you think would be helpful for me to know?'

Paraphrase

The purpose of paraphrasing is to demonstrate that you are listening and that you understand what is being communicated — as though holding a mirror to the discussion. Protégés appreciate knowing that they have been heard accurately, and this serves to prime the discussion pump.

There are four types of paraphrasing:

1. Restatement. In your own words, rather than the protégé's, state a condensed version of what the protégé said. Don't simply parrot or repeat the protégé's exact words; this communicates that you heard the protégé's statement, but not that you understood it.

2. General to specific. If the protégé's statement is a generalization, you might paraphrase it in more specific terms by expanding on one part of the statement or by giving an example. By stating the specific, you show that you understand the general.

3. Specific to general. If the protégé's statement is specific, paraphrase by stating a generalization or principle. By formulating a broader response, you indicate not only that you understand the protégé's statement, but also that the protégé's statement can, in fact, be generalized.

4. Restatement in opposite terms. Convey that you understand the meaning of the protégé's statement by restating it in opposite terms. For example, if the protégé says that a manager should do something, you can restate by saying that the manager should not do the opposite.

Consider the following statement: 'Effective auditing requires the auditor to have a special kind of cautious optimism.' As mentor, you might paraphrase this statement in any of the following ways:

> **Restatement:**
> 'You are saying that the auditor should be open but still careful.'

> **General to specific:**
> 'An auditor should carefully check every entry.'

> **Specific to general:**
> 'Sounds as though you think auditing is complex.'

> **Restatement in opposite terms:**
> 'You mean that the auditor should not be negative and overly suspicious.'

Paraphrasing encourages protégés to say more because they know they have been understood. An important point to remember is to look for a sign that the protégé agrees with your interpretation. If no sign is given, either verbal or nonverbal, ask the protégé whether you've paraphrased the statement accurately. If you make mistakes without checking, then you are demonstrating misunderstanding, which will fog the discussion and dampen the learning climate.

One last point on paraphrasing: Notice in the examples above that each sentence ends in a period. The goal of paraphrasing is to mirror or reflect your understanding, not to ask a question or make an exclamation. Make certain your inflection turns down, not up. Asking a question puts you in control. Making a explanatory statement puts you in control. Your goal is to leave the protégé in control and simply mirror what is he or she is communicating.

Summarize

Summarizing is similar to paraphrasing. The difference is that the goal of paraphrasing is to *mirror* the *meaning* to check for understanding, whereas the goal of summarizing is to synthesize to check for understanding. You synthesize by condensing the meaning of the protégé's comments into a sentence or two (or, if the comments were lengthy, into a paragraph) and repeating the synthesized information as a summary.

Summarizing typically begins with such phrases as:

'In other words . . . '

'What you're saying is that . . . '

'In summary, you think that. . . .'

Be careful about how you use certain phrases when summarizing. For example, too many uses of a catchphrase such as 'What I hear you saying is . . .' can begin to sound mechanical and condescending.

Extend

The purpose of extending is to add scope or depth to a protégé's comments. If what you add matches the spirit of what the protégé said, it not only communicates understanding but also enriches or expands understanding. Both technical information and information about personal views and feelings can be extended.

Technical information refers to building on the factual content of the protégé's comment. An example might be, 'You make a good point about the auditor's role in analyzing the corporation's financial statement. In addition, the auditor needs to ensure that all current regulations are met.'

Information about personal views and feelings is what a learner says about herself during the discussion. You can add to this kind of information, but do so with care. It is a very powerful method for demonstrating deep understanding, but it is also quite difficult to do convincingly and effectively. Extending in this way requires you to empathize strongly with the protégé. Here are two examples of what a mentor might say when extending personal information:

'So you advised your colleague to sue. I was once in exactly the same position. I supervised the EEO function of human resources, and. . . .'

'I agree. After I recovered from the initial shock of my father's Alzheimer's disease, I felt lonely and angry as well.'

Use Gestures and Body Stance

Your nonverbal behavior can prime the pump of discussion and contribute to a positive learning environment by helping to communicate your understanding. Conversely, certain nonverbal behaviors can have a detrimental effect: shaking your head in disapproval, rolling your eyes to the ceiling, frowning, or suddenly moving forward in your chair. These may convey a negative judgment and make the protégé less inclined to take risks.

An appropriate gesture is to nod your head or say 'uh-huh' to indicate understanding and encourage further dialogue. But don't overdo either of these cues or the protégé may feel that you are trying to manipulate the discussion rather than simply listening and encouraging.

DOS AND DON'TS FOR DIALOGUES

Dialogues are interpersonal crucibles for blending facts, figures, and feelings to concoct acumen and understanding. Dialogues are most powerful when you

- listen,

- do not teach,

- allow disagreement,

- create a warm, encouraging climate,

- are aware of the learning that is taking place,

- work as hard to learn from protégés as you hope they do from you, and

- do not pressure protégés to answer or behave as you think they should.

Above all, be authentic. Just be yourself while setting the tone, asking questions, and summing up discussions with your protégé rather than doing anything artificial or manipulative to keep the give-and-take going.

Discussions are opportunities for protégés to enhance their learning, not for the mentor to teach. Stay out of the way as much as possible to let the protégé do his or her own thinking. Try not to dominate the discussion. You need not comment on everything the protégé says. Sometimes a simple 'Good!' or 'Thank you' is best.

Jack Gamble on Dialogues
(Mentoring in Action Revisited)

Jack took another stab at the issue. "How does he react when you get stern and serious?"

"I'm not sure," Tracy responded.

Jack tried again. "Let me ask it this way: If I asked Adam to candidly describe you when the two of you talk about his performance, what words would he use?"

Tracy's demeanor began to change. It was as if the wheels of wisdom were turning in her head.

"He would say I was relentlessly patient." She was still half lost in thought.

"What else?"

Tracy responded with near excitement in her voice. "He would not describe me as tough, demanding, or disciplined."

Jack sensed that she was solving her own issue. Again, he paused before raising another question. He knew instinctively that pace was everything when insight was the goal. "So, what do you think should be your next step?"

Tracy began to outline steps: a serious conversation, a performance plan, short-term goals with clear feedback, supervision with a shorter leash, and, above all, less understanding and more discipline. Jack offered a few ideas, but mostly affirmation and encouragement. They parted with an agreement to revisit the issue in a few days. ■

"Real isn't how you are made," said the Skin Horse. "It's a thing that happens to you. . . . It doesn't happen all at once, you become. It takes a long time. That's why it doesn't often happen to people who break easily, or have sharp edges, or who have to be carefully kept."
— Margery Williams,
The Velveteen Rabbi

CHAPTER 13

For the Protégé

GETTING YOUR FEET WET
WITHOUT WORRYING ABOUT DROWNING

When we left off from our last 'For the Protégé' section, Sage was saying to you . . .

"Remember the other part . . . YOU have a responsibility to Dale. Now, go ahead and talk about it!"

"Oh, and Dale . . . there is one other goal I have for this experience. I want to do everything I can to make this a great mentoring experience for you."

Dale looks surprised and noticeably pleased. He responds awkwardly, but is obviously moved. You suddenly sense this relationship just got bumped up to a higher level.

"You're doing a great job. This is going to work out! Don't you think?"

Dale asks a few questions about your background with mentors, your reaction to this situation, ways to make this a good experience, potential interpersonal mine fields the two of you might encounter. The conversation seems to be going okay. Then, Dale shares a rather open, and surprisingly honest rendition of a former mentor who seemed to make every mentoring mistake in the book. Then, "What are *your* biggest fears about this relationship?" gets shot at you, like an arrow from an expert archer.

"Ohmygod," you think to yourself. "If I duck this question, I'll sound calloused. If I answer as frankly as I think Dale wants, I'll sound like wimp."

"You've got to get your feet wet sooner or later. Take a chance. Tell Dale exactly what you are feeling."

"Well, uh, uh . . . to tell you the truth . . . actually, I do have a few concerns . . . I wouldn't call them fears . . . actually, I would. You're going to write an

evaluation on me at the end of this assignment. That tells me I need to always show you my best side. And I also know that if I'm going to learn anything, I'm going to look pretty stupid sometimes."

Dale takes a deep breath and looks straight at you. You feel your heart racing, as if it just left the starting blocks of a fifty-yard dash. Dale suddenly smiles and thanks you for your candor. It seems he has been worried about the same issue.

"See what I told you . . . candor is always the best policy!"

As you describe your concerns in more detail in response to his gentle probing, Dale listens intently to your responses. In fact, there are awkward pauses at times, separating your answers from Dale's next question. This is certainly different from other mentoring sessions. You are much more accustomed to rapid-fire interrogation in which the last few words of your answer are drowned out by the first few words of the next question. Dale seems sincerely intent on doing a good job, taking the long way around before getting into the heart of your discussion. In fact, Dale's wind-up seems to take so long you begin to wonder about the efficiency of this approach.

"Let Dale know you are eager to get into the thick of the mentoring session. Dale needs your signal now."

"Dale, I'm feeling really excited about how this session is going. I'd like to throw out a problem I'm having and get your thoughts on how I might handle it."

Dale seems pleased with your enthusiasm to get things going.

Part IV

Gifting:
THE MAIN EVENT

Gifting

THE MAIN EVENT

I grew up on a small farm in South Georgia. I made most of my annual spending money mowing lawns in the summertime. (I think the concept of an allowance was not invented until 1962 — after I left home!) I got a dollar for a regular yard and two dollars for a large yard. My grandparents had a two-dollar yard. I always got excited when it was time to mow their yard because there weren't a lot of two-dollar yards where I lived.

In the summer of 1954 we had a major drought, the kind of rainless condition that makes yards go into a don't-grow, just-survive mode. I was looking at a bleak school year economically. Toward the end of that summer, my grandmother called and said, "Chip, I want you to mow my yard." I was thrilled! I don't think it really needed mowing, but she seemed to sense my cash shortage and came to my rescue. I mowed her yard and met her on the back porch to get my two dollars. Instead she handed me a five-dollar bill and said the most generous words I had ever heard: "Keep the change!" It changed my relationship with my grandmother — and I kept the change until she passed away at eighty-four.

After you extend the invitation to the mentoring process (through surrendering) and establish the relationship (through accepting), the platform is set for the main event: gifting. Essentially, the protégé is in the presence of the mentor for the gifts the mentor can offer. However, the way this encounter is managed can make a dramatic difference in the quality of both the learning and its retention.

Gifting is an expression of generosity. It is different from giving. 'Giving' often implies some reciprocal toll; 'gifting' is the bestowing of assets without any expectation of return. The spirit of gifting changes the nature of the relationship from guilt-based indebtedness to joy-driven partnership. And the alliance of mentor and protégé is far healthier when the pleasure of teaching exactly matches the enchantment of learning. Why is this so?

Relationships are healthier when there is some reciprocity or balance — not perfectly fifty-fifty, but some appropriate level of fairness. Most learner-takers, however, feel indebted to their mentor-givers: 'She gives so much, and I have nothing to give in return.' This is how guilt, liability, and obligation get started. Such anxieties, no matter how subliminal, get in the way of effective development. The learner has no tangible way to balance the relationship, at least in the short run. So it is important for the mentor to show that she has been amply rewarded by the opportunity to mentor and the pleasure inherent in the process. Reciprocity is the mentor's saying indirectly to the protégé, 'My payment is the sheer joy I get from seeing you grow and learn. You owe me nothing.'

The next seven chapters will explore several dimensions of gifting. The opening chapter in this part zeroes in on the most frequent gift associated with mentoring: advice. The challenge mentors face is how to deliver advice without surfacing protégé resistance. The next chapter examines another important gift, that of feedback. Learner motivation is enhanced by the protégé's perceiving a valued purpose in the learning. It is incumbent on the mentor to communicate the rationale for what is to be learned. Balance is another important contribution to the learning process. A section on mentor gifts would not be complete without a piece on storytelling. Stories have been the tools of learner discovery since the campfire was invented. The second-to-last chapter addresses perhaps the most important gift of the mentor: passion. Few attitudes fuel the excitement of a learner more than to witness her or his mentor enthused by the process of learning and zealous about prospects of protégé growth. Finally, we look at this phase of mentoring from the protégé's side, a perspective that also shows how great mentors deal with the guilt and gratitude that accompanies gifting.

CHAPTER 14
Avoiding Thin Ice
THE GIFT OF ADVICE

Someone once asked famed South Carolina head football coach Lou Holtz what he considered to be the toughest part of his job. With his typical 'aw shucks' charm, he finessed the question but ultimately communicated that one of the hardest parts was 'teaching lessons that stay taught.'

Mentors have a similar challenge. Mentoring can involve everything from chalkboard teaching to spirited discussion to circulation of relevant articles, but one of its most challenging parts is giving advice. Recall the last time someone said, 'Let me give you a little advice!' No doubt it quickly put you into a defensive posture.

Psychologists remind us that we all have authority hang-ups of varying severity. So does your protégé — and the protégé's resistance to advice creates the challenge in teaching lessons that stay taught. As one frustrated supervisor commented, 'I tell 'em what they ought to do, but it seems to go in one ear and out the other!' Giving Advice Without Getting Resistance

Advice giving works only in the context of learning — that is, when you are offering advice because you believe that the protégé's performance will be improved if his knowledge or skill is enhanced. This is important, because for advice giving truly to work, you must be ready for the protégé to choose not to take your advice. If the protégé has no real choice about honoring your advice, then you should simply give a directive and be done with it. Couching your requirement as advice is manipulative and will only foster distrust and resentment.

There are four steps for making your advice giving more powerful and more productive. Pay attention to the sequence; it is crucial to your success.

Step 1:
Clearly State the Performance Problem or Learning Goal

Begin your advice giving by letting the protégé know the focus or intent of your mentoring. Suppose you're offering advice about improving the performance of a new skill the protégé is trying to master. You might say, 'George, I wanted to talk with you about the fact that although your last quarter call rate was up, your sales were down 20 percent.' For advice giving to work, you must be very specific and clear in your statement. Ambiguity clouds the conversation and risks leaving the protégé more confused than enlightened.

Stating the focus — an important coaching technique in general — helps sort out the form and content of the advice. Is the problem something that is not working or something that is lacking? Stated differently, is the occasion for the advice a skill deficiency (requiring mentoring) or a will deficiency (requiring coaching)? Being clear up front about the purpose of your advice can help focus your scattergun thoughts into laserlike advice.

Step 2: Make Sure You Agree on the Focus

If what seems to you a performance challenge is seen by the protégé as something else, your advice will be viewed as overcontrolling or smothering. Make sure the protégé is as eager to improve as you are to see him improve. You may learn that the protégé has already determined what to do and has little need for your advice. Your goal is to hear the protégé say something like, 'Yes, I've been concerned about that as well.'

What do you do if you think there is something the protégé needs to learn but the protégé is unwilling? Many lessons get 'taught' (but not learned) under this scenario. As Abraham Lincoln said, "A person convinced against his will is of the same opinion still."

Take a broader perspective. If a performance deficiency needs to be remedied, have available objective information that you both can examine. If all else fails, wait until the protégé shows more readiness to learn. To abuse the adage: You can lead a horse to water, but you can't make him think. Although protégés are by no means horses, they can sometimes be as stubborn.

Step 3: Ask Permission to Give Advice

This is the most important step. Your goal at this point is twofold:

1. to communicate advice without eliciting protégé resistance, and

2. to keep ownership of the challenge with the protégé.

This does not mean asking, 'May I have your permission to . . . ?' Rather, you might say, 'I have some ideas on how you might improve if that would be helpful to you.'

I know what you're thinking. What fool is going to tell her boss, 'I'm not interested in your advice!'? Most protégés will heed your advice, of course, and many will be grateful for it. But remember, your goal is to communicate in a way that minimizes the protégé's being controlled or coerced — especially the perception of being controlled.

The essence of resistance is control. None of us is thrilled to be told what to do, and some are more defiant than others. So what do you do if, despite your best efforts, you sense protégé resistance?

Two rules:

1. **Never resist resistance.** Back off; take a second. Examine your stance, tone, choice of words to see whether you might be inadvertently fueling the resistance.

2. **Name the issue and take the hit!** Sometimes, simply stating in a low-key, nonconfrontational way how you see the situation — while assuming culpability — can drain the tension. You could say something like this: 'I could be wrong on this, but I worry that I may have come on too strong just now and implied that I was commanding you. That was not my intent.'

Step 4: State Your Advice in First Person Singular

Phrases like 'you ought to' quickly raise resistance! By keeping your advice in the first-person singular — 'what I found helpful' or 'what worked for me' — helps eliminate the shoulds and ought-tos. The protégé will hear such advice unscreened by defensiveness or resistance.

A DRAMA IN FOUR STEPS

Now let's put the steps together in a role play to illustrate the tone and technique of advice giving. Billy is a new reservations clerk for Mayday Airlines; Kay is his section leader. Mayday has just installed a new reservation system. Some of the features are similar to the old system on which Billy was an expert. Some of the steps can be done several ways. Kay has observed that Billy follows a mass-pull-sort approach on the new system, as he did on the old. She believes Billy's efficiency would improve if he used a pull-mass-spread-sort approach.

Kay: "Billy, I've been impressed with your work. I've also noticed that your pace seems to slow when you use the mass-pull-sort approach."

Billy: "Yes, I must admit I find doing it that way a lot more comfortable. I guess using it for ten years has something to do with it."

Kay: "I know exactly what you mean. It was tough for me to let go of some of the older approaches, especially when I was evaluated on speed and shifting to a new approach would slow me down at first. I've been watching how you do it, and I have a suggestion that might help improve your speed over time."

Billy: "Shoot. I'm all ears if it helps me get faster."

Kay: "I found that the pull-mass-spread-sort approach, while awkward at first, gave me a lot more control over the reservation fields and was actually easier after a day or so than mass-pull-sort. I'll be honest with you — if someone had just told me it would be easier, I wouldn't have believed it. But I tried it and was really surprised. You might want to try it yourself."

Billy: "Sounds all right. I'll give it a try."

And they all lived happily ever after, of course.

Giving advice is like playing pinball: Only by pushing and pulling can you encourage the ball to go in a new direction and increase your score. But too much pushing and pulling can cause a tilt and stop the game. Effective mentors recognize the challenge of 'teaching so it stays taught' and meet that challenge by coupling their wisdom with sensitivity. They keep the ball in play as long as they can by judicious application of pushes and pulls, nudges and bumps, building the score — the protégé's competence.

> "There is no human problem which could not be solved if people would simply do as I advise."
> — Gore Vidal

Jack Gamble on Advice Giving
(Mentoring In Action Revisited)

Jack waited to make sure she had no more to say about the subject. "How can I help?" he asked, not wanting to assume anything yet about whether his assistance was required.

Tracy looked straight at him. "I guess I need you to be a sounding board, and maybe give me some ideas on how to get him fired up — or fired."

"What do you think the problem is, based on what you know?" asked Jack.

"His morale is lousy. When I try to talk with him about his performance, his nonverbals are rather patronizing, like he's offended that I raised the issue."

Jack thought for a minute. "I can see that would be a tough nut to crack. I've never been really comfortable dealing with negative performers. It always makes me feel anxious if I have to get tough with an employee. I can see — "

"But you still manage to get them turned around," interrupted Tracy.

Jack could see that Tracy thought he had some magical secret he had kept to himself. "You believe there's a special technique that maybe you've missed."

"Yes, I suppose I do, in a way. You make it look easy. I remember when you had to terminate Edsel Joiner. The guy ended up thanking you for it!"

Jack did not respond for a while. Tracy suddenly felt awkward, as though she had allowed her stream of emotion to overflow its banks. Then, with unusual emotion in his voice, Jack said, "That was the scariest thing I've ever done since I came to work here." They both sat in silence. ∎

CHAPTER 15

Reporting on Blind Spots
THE GIFT OF FEEDBACK

Ken Blanchard is credited with labeling the word 'feedback' as the 'breakfast of champions.' Ken was giving us more than a clever sound bite by borrowing from the tag line from the Wheaties® cereal ad. When you dissect the word into its parts — 'feed' and 'back' — you get the intended connotation of feedback as a tool for nurturing wisdom. Think of it as learning fuel. And given that breakfast is the most important meal of the day (we literally break fast), the symbolism is far more significant than calling it the 'supper of champions.'

How do you give feedback intended to fuel growth? Start by recognizing that while giving advice can surface resistance, giving feedback can stir up resentment. Advice is about expanding the scope of knowledge; feedback is about filling a blind spot. I'll illustrate with a true-life experience.

In the late sixties I served in Vietnam as an army infantry unit commander in the 82nd Airborne. Attached to my combat unit was an artillery officer who worked as the forward observer (FO) for the artillery unit in the rear that supported our field operations. This FO essentially served as the eyes for the gunner pulling the lanyard on the artillery piece. As rounds were fired several miles out, the FO observed their impact and, using a field radio, called in corrections to improve the accuracy of the next shot.

The FO never said, 'Lousy shot,' or 'Well, that was better than last week.' He would simply say, 'Drop one hundred meters,' or 'West one-fifty,' or 'Pay dirt!' This was feedback, not advice; the FO had a perspective the gunner needed and did not have.

There is one key difference between artillery feedback and mentoring feedback: Artillery feedback is not likely to make the recipient angry. Advice is expertise the protégé may have or could acquire. Resistance to advice is therefore about premature smartness — that is, 'You (the mentor) are telling me (the protégé) something you know that, in time, I can learn on my own.' But with feedback, the issue is this: 'You (the mentor) are telling me something you know that I will never learn on my own, and that irritates me.' The danger with advice is potential resistance; with feedback, it is potential resentment.

'But what about confirming feedback?' you may be thinking. 'Surely protégés won't resent feedback telling them that their efforts are on target.' To the protégé, however, such well-intentioned confirmation can seem patronizing. The unspoken reply to your 'This report you wrote is complete and effective' may be 'What gives you the right to tell me this?'

Once I had an acquaintance who was legally blind (today we would call her visually challenged). She was not self-conscious about her challenge. At a dinner party, a close friend asked her, "What is the hardest part about being blind?" She replied, "When people assist me, I sometimes cannot tell if the help is for my preservation or their pretension." Confirming feedback should contain the same level of care as corrective feedback.

SERVING THE BREAKFAST OF CHAMPIONS

How does a mentor bestow a gift that by its nature reminds the protégé of his inability to see it? Below are four steps that can make giving feedback more powerful and more productive. The steps are numbered because the order is vital to their effectiveness.

Step 1: Create a Climate of Identification — 'I'm Like You'

A key factor in giving feedback is the protégé's embarrassment over some blind spot. Granted, 'embarrassment' might at times be too strong a label for the protégé's feelings, but at other times it is not strong enough. In any event, the mentor can enhance the protégé's receptivity by creating a climate of identification. Make comments that have an 'I'm like you — that is, not perfect or flawless' message. This need not be a major production — just a sentence or two to establish rapport.

Step 2: State the Rationale for the Feedback

In addition to overcoming embarrassment about the blind spot, the protégé will need to understand the context of the feedback. Help the protégé gain a clear sense of why the feedback is being given. Ensure that there is a clear perspective for making sense of the feedback. When you give feedback, you never want to make the protégé wonder, 'Why is she telling me this?' or 'How in the world can I benefit from this?'

Step 3: Assume You're Giving Yourself the Feedback

Besides being clear and empathetic, feedback must be straightforward and honest. This does not mean it must be blunt or cruel; it means that the protégé should not be left wondering, 'What did she not tell me that I needed to hear?' Trust is born of clean communication. Think of your goal this way: How would you deliver the feedback if you were giving it to yourself? Take your cues from your own preferences; give feedback as you would receive it.

Step 4: Ask for What You Gave — Feedback

There is one action you can take that will both help you improve your mentoring and level the playing field in the protégé's mind: Ask for feedback from the protégé. Let the protégé know that you want the feedback process to work both ways. From time to time the forward observer attached to my army infantry unit would ask the gunner for feedback on his FO technique. The gunner was given a shot at calling in a few corrections of his own, so to speak. It gave our unit confidence to know that the dialogue was a two-way street.

EATING YOUR OWN COOKING

When I was a college freshman I was exposed to a well-known communication model called the Johari Window, developed by Joe Luft and Harry Ingham. The instructor made the theory sound like a deep, mysterious concept. I thought it was a blinding glimpse of the obvious. However, years later I revisited the model and learned the instructor had failed to deliver the punch line — the cogent point — and made the model sound far shallower than its creators intended.

Here is a quick overview of the model, put in the setting of mentoring.

When mentor and protégé interact, there are things the protégé knows about the mentor, and there are things the protégé does not know about the mentor. Conversely, there are things the mentor knows about him or herself and things the mentor does not know about him or herself. If we put these two parts together, we get a 2 x 2 model (see figure 2 on next page) :

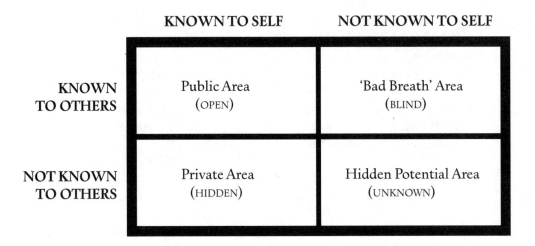

	KNOWN TO SELF	NOT KNOWN TO SELF
KNOWN TO OTHERS	Public Area (OPEN)	'Bad Breath' Area (BLIND)
NOT KNOWN TO OTHERS	Private Area (HIDDEN)	Hidden Potential Area (UNKNOWN)

FIGURE 2. THE JOHARI WINDOW

The 'Known to Others/Known to Self' cell is called our 'Public Area'—you know I'm from Texas, and I know I'm from Texas. The 'Known to Others/Not Known to Self' cell is called the 'Bad Breath Area'—things others know about you that they could tell you but haven't. The 'Not Known to Others/Known to Self' is our private area — secrets we have kept from others about ourselves. The 'Not Known to Others/Not Known to Self' represents our hidden or unknown potential — aspects of ourselves that neither we nor others know, simply because we have never been in or assumed a position to demonstrate them.

When the grad student instructor presented the Johari Window to our class, this is where he stopped. But there is more . . . much more. The point he failed to make is that understanding comes through increasing our public area — in a mentoring relationship, the part known to both mentor and protégé. How does the mentor move the 'Known to Others' boundary downward and the 'Known to Self' boundary to the right, to enlarge the Public Area?

The horizontal boundary of the Public Area (line A) can be pushed downward through disclosure. If you reveal or disclose areas formerly private to now be public, you increase the size of that cell in the 'Known to Others/Not Know to Others' dimension. Line B is moved to the right by soliciting feedback. If you ask your protégé for feedback and it is given, things formerly 'not known to self' are revealed. The idea is to use both methods — disclosure and feedback — to move the boundaries in both directions. Remember, understanding comes from a having a large Public Area . . . emanating from knowledge both you and your protégé share.

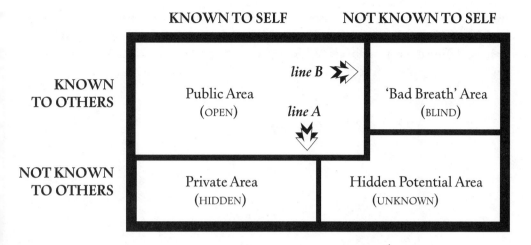

FIGURE 3. EXPANDING THE PUBLIC AREA

A BREAKFAST INVITATION

I promised you a good punch line to the story. It is this: Before we can solicit feedback, we must start with disclosure. Before you can get helpful feedback from the protégé, you must be willing to be open and disclosing about sharing parts of yourself the protégé might not know.

For a true-life example, take Bruce Fritch. Bruce has always been an important mentor to me. While we don't have as much contact today as when we lived in the same town, he continues to show a keen interest in my professional development. My best learning jump-starts come with our super-frank professional discussions. And I can hear and value his 'no training wheels' feedback because he insists on reciprocity — he solicits just as diligently as he delivers!

Bruce solicits my feedback by first cataloging some of the personal and professional 'warts' he is working to remove. This gives me a gauge on how open he'd like our conversation to be. His courageous plunge gives me the confidence I need to solicit equally candid feedback. While the outcome is usually not without some discomfort, it is always extremely accurate and helpful. Together, we get great nourishment from the breakfast of champions.

It is instructive that the word 'feedback' starts with the word 'feed.' Truly the best gap filling happens in the spirit of feeding or nurturing. It is also fitting that the word 'advice' probably came from the Latin word 'concilium,' meaning 'to call together.' Our words 'counsel' and 'consult' have the same origin. If we blend these archaic definitions of feedback and advice, we get a perfect description of a learning partnership — 'to feed together.'

"Honest criticism is hard to take, particularly from a relative, a friend, an acquaintance, or a stranger."
— Franklin P. Jones

CHAPTER 16
Linking Proficiency to Purpose
THE GIFT OF FOCUS

Mrs. Ridley and I got into a big argument in twelfth-grade English class. We had just gotten back our test papers from a pop quiz on our understanding of the ancient classic *Beowolf.* One of the test questions was "What were the main ingredients of the pie served at the king's banquet?" I had had no clue when I took the test and left the question blank.

"How on earth is knowing about the ingredients of this pie going to help us later in life?" I curtly asked Mrs. Ridley. My irritated insolence stood in stark contrast with her warm patience as she skillfully deflated my unexpected uproar. I don't remember what she gave as an explanation. I just remember privately wondering why suddenly, at age seventeen, I was interested in future relevance, something I had simply taken for granted a few years earlier. I now know it was a sign of emerging adulthood.

Remember, adult learning and child learning are different when it comes to focus. Children are patient with delayed application and the promise that 'someday you'll find this helpful.' Adults question the worth of knowing the ingredients of the pie at the king's banquet. As adults, we want real-time relevance and immediate application. And, if the tie to usefulness is unclear or absent, our motivation drops and our attention drifts.

Proper protégé motivation is vital to protégé learning. Motivation is surfaced in part by linking what is being learned with a grander purpose. Call it 'competence with a cause,' to suggest that as learners we need the 'why' as much as we need the 'how.' We want our pursuit to be in the direction of some desirable end-point, as Peter Senge wrote in *The Fifth Discipline*: "Shared vision is vital for the learning organization because it provides focus and energy for learning. Innovative learning occurs only when people are striving to accomplish something that matters deeply to them."

> "The future belongs to those who believe the beauty of their dreams."
>
> — Eleanor Roosevelt

FOCUSING ON PURPOSE

The Ritz-Carlton Hotel Company is known for extraordinary elegance and world-class customer service. Winner of the 1992 and 1999 Malcolm Baldrige National Quality Award, it achieved distinction not just through great quality but consistently great quality — across all hotels and all properties. A key part of the Ritz-Carlton consistency comes through a clear vision: "We are ladies and gentlemen serving ladies and gentlemen." Every employee from general manager to housekeeper is clear on that vision as well as its specific implications for their role.

As clear and powerful as their vision is — and the twenty customer-service practices that accompany it — it is useless unless it is kept alive and fresh. It becomes no more than a clever billfold-sized, tri-fold, laminated card unless it serves as the grounding and touchstone for every action and all decisions. When Ritz-Carlton employees do 'line-up,' a ten-minute stand-up meeting in every department at every shift change, it includes an articulation of 'what we learned today that would impact the guests' experience tomorrow.' Learning is tied to purpose. Every new employee orientation begins with the vision and values, not with policies and procedures.

Nordstrom uses its employee empowerment policy — "Use your good judgment in all situations" — as the basis for many of their learning programs. "Learning at Nordstrom," says one department manager at their flagship store in downtown Seattle, "is all aimed at helping associates think like owners. Good judgment comes from good know-how." Springfield ReManufacturing goes a step further. Employees are taught business literacy skills. "We want our employees to know the skills needed to run their jobs just like it was their own business. If they don't know the impact of their everyday decisions on the profitability of the business, how can we expect them to not be wasteful or inefficient?" says CEO Jack Stack.

Why before What and How

Mentoring with focus means taking time to help link emerging acumen with an exciting aim. It might not be the global vision of the corporation, like the forward-thinking Ritz-Carlton, but rather some short-term objective of the unit. Adult learning guru Fredric Margolis says, "When giving learning direction, always let the 'why' come before the 'what' or the 'how.'" The crux of Margolis's point is that learners can psychologically and emotionally hear the 'what' or 'how' in a fundamentally different way if it is preceded by the rationale.

The rationale is always stated from the protégé's perspective, not the mentor's, or the unit's, or the organization's. Here is the difference:

From the Organization's Perspective:

'When interviewing someone for a job, you may or may not choose to reveal certain things about yourself or the organization. At Acme, we believe you should know in advance what you will reveal before you begin an interview. In a moment I will provide you an opportunity to practice revealing information.'

From the Protégé's Perspective:

'When interviewing someone for a job, you may or may not choose to reveal certain things about yourself or the organization. What is important is that you feel comfortable and competent in revealing certain information to the person being interviewed. This feeling comes with experience. The more we risk, the better we become at taking risks. In a moment you will have the opportunity to practice revealing information.'

The rationale should communicate a personal reason for learning as well as a professional reason. The reason presented should be one with which the protégé can identify, one that makes logical as well as emotional sense. It should not be a justification by the mentor in terms of the needs of the unit or the organization.

Grounding Summaries with Substance

Grounding is all about creating a foundation for learning. Grounding lends a bolstering sturdiness to new skills or knowledge. Think of the learning rationale as providing not only direction but roots as well. Building a foundation is by definition an initial act. However, foundations only support when they are maintained. An effective mentor will frequently circle back to the rationale and 'help the protégé touch the touchstone.' One way to do this is with a summary statement, such as 'Overall, this skill is vital to what we are working to accomplish because. . . .' Or you reinforce the foundation with a question: 'Tell me again the reason this learning is important?'

Adult learners need a sense of purpose to engage their enthusiasm. Wise mentors can bolster purposeful learning by using vision, objectives, and rationale to ensure growth has both direction (focus) and grounding (foundation). It is not the words we speak it is the strategy employed to elevate learning from simply a task to be accomplished to that of a grander cause and a nobler endeavor.

CHAPTER 17
The Bluebird's Secret
THE GIFT OF BALANCE

There's a bluebird house on an oak tree six feet from our bedroom window. The same pair of bluebirds comes each spring to build, populate, and empty a nest in it. This past spring, their parenting process caused me to reflect on how instructive bluebird flying lessons could be for mentors. Bluebirds don't just hatch eggs and depart. They act as mentors in getting a young bird from the security of the birdhouse to the serenity of flight.

Effective mentoring is especially crucial in this era of rapid change and increasing organizational complexity. Employees who don't continue to grow will be unable to cope, adapt, and succeed. Those who wait for the next opening in a much-needed training class may be quickly left behind. In times like these, the mentor becomes a key source for real-time employee learning. But combining an in-charge role with an 'in-sight' goal calls for balance — and that's where the bluebirds come in.

FINDING THE TEACHABLE MOMENT

How does the bluebird know when its fast-growing offspring is ready to be pushed from the nest? Bluebirds have genetically coded weaning instincts and an innate sense of timing. They watch for certain subtle signs of maturity: restlessness, wing strength, the eagerness of the infant's lunge toward the birdhouse exit even when there's no worm dangling from mama's beak, and a whole bunch of other stuff they haven't told the bird researchers.

One key to their attentiveness is the way they take different viewpoints. Bluebird parents often perch some distance away and call out to the baby bluebird, as though to gauge reaction time — how fast does Junior respond to the chirp? A parent bluebird might perch atop the birdhouse and peer down through the entrance hole. While it would obviously be easier to observe from inside, the bluebird knows that to get a true picture the comfortable and familiar close-up examination must be balanced with views from more dangerous and diverse angles and conditions.

Baby bluebirds and protégés need teachable moments. One of the chief complaints protégés make about their mentors is, 'He was not on hand when I really needed him.' This key, often brief opportunity is sometimes called 'the teachable moment.' The timing of this moment is important: It's a combination of the learner's readiness to learn, the quickness with which learning can be applied, and the special conditions likely to foster or support learning.

So what should a mentor do to match teaching with timing? And how does the mentor demonstrate the right amount of attention? Too much attention can leave the protégé feeling smothered; too little can make her feel abandoned.

- Stay vigilant for every opportunity to foster discovery. Whenever you communicate with the protégé, ask yourself, 'Is there learning that can be derived from this?'

- Keep a lookout for signs of protégé apathy, boredom, or dullness, any of which may indicate a plateau in learning.

- Ask 'A' and listen for 'B.' For example, ask the question, 'How would you describe the challenge in your job?' but listen for the answer as if you had asked, 'How would you describe your growth or learning deficit in your job?' It is far easier for protégés to talk about being challenged or not being challenged than to discuss a learning deficit.

- From a distance, watch the protégé at work. As you watch your birdhouse from a distant railing, keep in mind that your goal is to determine whether it might be a good time to intervene as a mentor.

SUPPORT WITHOUT RESCUING

The morning the baby bluebird took that first clumsy flight from the birdhouse to the nearest bush, both parents were on hand for the occasion, proud and no doubt anxious. As the wobbly fledgling took a short, awkward burst of flight, one parent was in the tree nearby, providing comforting chirps of encouragement.

Suddenly, Taco (Bell), our black cat, came around the corner. Instantly, one of the parents flew within a few feet of Taco, distracting her long enough for the young bird to reach a limb safely out of reach. It was a beautiful display of courageous selflessness by the parent, vital and well-timed support — but the student pilot was still left to do his own flying.

Mentors provide support and encouragement as protégés work to transform shaky new skills into confident mastery. The challenges for all mentors are 'When does too much support become rescuing?' and 'When does too little support become a sign of callousness?' Most mentors are tempted to take help to the level of interference. Too often we say, 'Let me just show you how to do that!' when we should be asking, 'What do you think you should do next?'

The following assemble-it-yourself statement may help you find the right balance between helpful support and unhelpful rescue:

If I were really honest with myself, I would say I tend to offer help because:

- I don't want to see the protégé repeat mistakes I've made.

- I can't afford too many errors in the name of learning.

- I don't want to see the protégé hurt, embarrassed, disappointed, or discouraged.

- I need to show the protégé how competent I am.

- If I don't show the protégé how, he'll never learn or become competent.

If there is one lesson the bluebirds can offer, it is the living illustration of the teacher's courage to let the learner fail. Mentors, like parents, want learning to be painless, but most significant growth happens through the discomfort of grappling for skill. En route to walking and running, knees get skinned. The bluebird dived courageously at the menacing cat as the student pilot fluttered awkwardly down the backyard runway. The parent seemed to be protecting its youngster — and more: demonstrating bravery for it. Learners dare to risk when they see the teacher take risks.

Avoid Perfection

There is one point this book makes over and over: The greatest gift a mentor can give a protégé is to demonstrate authenticity and realness. Conversely, the highest barrier to learning is an environment laced with expectations of perfection and implications of 'Why can't you be as good as I am?' There's nothing wrong with mentors showing off to protégés, as long as what they are showing is their genuineness — clay feet and all. Consider the following suggestions:

- Tape your mentoring sessions to see if they contain controlling language: 'I want you to . . . ,' 'You should . . . ,' or the patronizing royal 'we,' as in 'Now we must take our medicine.'

- Listen for whether you are taking as many interpersonal risks as the protégé in being real and open. Do you sound like an expert or a fellow learner? Would the protégé hear you as a schoolmarm or as an experienced colleague?

- Eliminate anything that may communicate power or distance. Mentoring from behind a desk can be far more intimidating than sitting at a forty-five-degree angle without barriers. Role or position power can be an obstacle when learning is the objective. Take steps to literally and symbolically minimize its effect.

- Be open to alternative views and unique interpretations. The path to excellence zigs and zags between extreme views. Help the protégé refine her view by honoring the extreme, while asking questions to encourage the discovery of a balanced, more effective position.

- Take the learning seriously, but not yourself. Laugh *with* your protégé, never at his or her mistakes. An occasional 'I made that same mistake' can melt learner apprehension and promote the risk taking needed to learn.

Our bluebirds are empty-nesters at the moment. Their fledgling has no doubt joined the world of adult bluebirds and is out hunting tasty bugs, dodging curious cats, and perhaps serving as the flight instructor for a newer generation. Like the bluebirds, the final gift of the mentor is to allow the protégé the freedom to find her own way.

Mentor Scale and Balance

The Mentor Scale can be helpful in examining the issue of balance. Below are a few cautions based on your score on the Mentor Scale.

Sociability

LOW: You may have a propensity to leave the protégé feeling abandoned. Provide more attention. Don't be so quick to mentor and run. Demonstrate your interest in and concern for your protégé.

HIGH: You may have a tendency to smother the protégé by over assisting. Remember that too much help can be as great a liability as too little. Back off a bit and give the protégé a wonderful opportunity: the chance to fail, and thus to learn.

Dominance

LOW: You may leave the protégé feeling betrayed. When he gets no guidance at all, the protégé can feel alone and anxious — especially early in the relationship. Let self-direction happen, but don't abdicate. Hang in there with the learner until you conclude he has wings strong enough to fly on his own.

HIGH: You may have an inclination to rescue. Remember that growth comes through discovery and insight. Too much control can deprive the learner of the opportunity to find them on his own. Let go of the reins and give your protégé a bit more slack.

Openness

LOW: You may cause the protégé to feel anxious, particularly early in the relationship. Guarded behavior begets guarded behavior. Remember, your timidity, caution, and reserve will only amplify similar feelings in the protégé. Take interpersonal risks, lighten up, and communicate your feelings. It will help break the ice and relax your protégé.

HIGH: When you are too open too soon, you can make the protégé feel apprehensive. You set a standard that learners may think they are incapable of or unwilling to model and match. Openness and vulnerability are positive attributes in a mentoring relationship. However, too much too soon can be overwhelming. ■

"Well-timed silence hath more eloquence than speech."
— M. T. Tupper

CHAPTER 18
Once Upon a Time
THE GIFT OF STORY

People are different, son. They don't all see things the same way." It was the opening line of my dad's effort to help me cope with the challenges of learning about relationships. He continued: "It reminds me of the comic strip 'Mutt and Jeff.'" The strip was one of my daddy's favorites. In the late 1950s it was one of everybody's favorites.

"Mutt and Jeff were playing a game of golf and having a great time," Dad told me. "As they approached the ninth tee, Mutt says to Jeff, "You know, Jeff, if everybody saw like I did, everybody would want my wife." Jeff saw this as the perfect time to bring his star-struck buddy back to reality. "I don't know about that Mutt," Jeff says. "If everybody saw like I did, nobody would want your wife." They both have a great laugh! I suddenly gained new insight into relationships. His corny story helped me understand how important it was to try to see things through the eyes of another.

STORYTELLING 101

People love stories. They love to tell them and they love to hear them. A really good story makes a campfire worth lighting, a cocktail party worth attending, and a reunion worth holding. A story can evoke tears and laughter. A good story can touch something familiar in each of us and, yet, show us something new about our lives, our world, ourselves.

Stories can also be powerful tools for mentoring. They can reach resistant protégés in ways that well-crafted advice may not. Unlike straightforward advice or feedback, stories have a way of circumventing the mind's logic to capture the imagination. As such, they are great gifts when delivered with care, content, and caution.

Most stories are either crafted or chosen. The crafted ones are 'baked from scratch'; the chosen ones, like Dad's Mutt and Jeff story are 're-crafted'—in other words, tailored to fit the mentor, the protégé, and the learning objective. The objective is paramount. Stories without purpose obviously lack relevance, but they also tend to lack charm.

Whether a mentor chooses to craft or re-craft a story, several key steps are involved. The first step is to clarify a story's purpose. Here's a checklist of questions to ask yourself:

- What key learning points do I hope to convey with a story?

- By using a story, am I indulging in irrelevant fantasy? Is the point best communicated by analogy?

- Is my protégé likely to appreciate the point if it's conveyed by a story? Or is he or she likely to be literal minded and view stories as 'much ado about nothing'?

- How do I convey the story so it comes alive and achieves its purpose?

Most mentors can learn to tell stories well, but some may find storytelling so challenging that they prefer to use other approaches. If you decide to incorporate a story into your mentoring discussions, you may find it helpful to structure your story around the following elements: the context, the challenge, and the climax.

The Context: Painting the Background

The story's context establishes the setting or scene. It's the 'once upon a time' part that invites the protégé into the story. In a sense, the context allows the protégé to become a witnesses to the visions of the storyteller.

A story should start with a transition that uses words or cues — such as a long pause — to signify that a story is beginning. Listeners shouldn't wonder why you are telling them what you're telling them, and they shouldn't be asking themselves, 'Where does this fit in?' My dad prefaced his instructive story on relationships with, "People are different, son. They don't all see things the same way. It reminds me of the comic strip 'Mutt and Jeff.'"

After the transition, it's important to create a realistic backdrop. Often, a story takes more time to relate than it takes to happen, so you should allow enough time to set the scene. Dad's story had a setting that communicated the tone of the story: "Mutt and Jeff were playing a game of golf and having a great time. All of a sudden Mutt said to Jeff, 'You know, Jeff, if everybody saw like I did, everybody would want my wife.'"

Even well-told stories often violate grammatical rules. They commonly shift between the past tense and the present. The past tense tells what happened; the present tense is acted out.

When creating the context of your story, ask yourself the following questions:

- What do I want the protégé to feel?

- How can I build a sense of adventure, mystery, suspense, joy, or invitation?

- Will my protégé be able to visualize the scene I have in my mind?

- Will my protégé be able to identify with or relate to the story and the picture I've planned?

The Challenge: Creating the Proper Tension

A good story should contain a challenge, which can also be described as 'dissonance.' To communicate dissonance, it's important to create a dilemma that the protégé can identify with. Even my dad's short story had a bit of tension when he said, "Jeff saw this as the perfect time to bring his star-struck buddy back to reality."

Once you've created a dilemma, you should describe in your story plan the challenge for each of the key characters using one sentence—for example, 'John's challenge is such-and-such. Sue's challenge is such and such.' This can help you keep things straight or 'manage' the story.

The following questions can help you create dissonance:

- What do I want the protégé to feel?

- How can I build a sense of concern, conflict, or suspense?

- Will the protégé be able to visualize the challenge or challenges the same way that I do?

- Will the dilemma create enough dissonance so that the protégé will desire a resolution?

The Climax: Insight through Resolution

The story's climax is essentially a punch line with a lesson. Of course, the lesson is usually longer than the typical punch line of a joke.

The climax is more than just an ending. It's a resolution that can be used as a tool for helping the protégé to learn. The storyteller instructs through resolution, and the protégé allows his or her need for resolution to lead to the learning. The climax must clearly fit the challenge and also carry the protégé in new and somewhat unexpected directions.

If a story were mapped out, the climax would reside on the other side of the gaps created by the challenge. It the listener leaps over the gaps, thus eliminating the dissonance, he or she experiences insight and learning. But the climax must be truly inviting, realistic, and relevant. If the climax or resolution is too routine or far-fetched, there is no insight. The protégé must be able to relate to and identify with how the story ends.

When creating the climax, ask yourself the following questions:

- Will the story's ending result in learning and achieve a mentoring goal? Is a story the best way to accomplish that with this protégé?

- Will the ending surprise, amuse, challenge, or amaze?

- Will the protégé view the ending as realistic and relevant?

- Will the protégé be able to envision several possible endings before the climax is revealed?

- Will the protégé gain insight and develop new attitudes, understanding, or skills from the resolution?

At the story's end, your protégé should say, 'I wouldn't have thought of that' or 'I wasn't expecting that.' He or she should also feel, upon reflection, that the story makes perfect sense.

PUTTING THE RIGHT SPIN ON THE TALE

Even a well-crafted story can fail to achieve its objectives if it isn't told well. Here are a few techniques and tips for effectively delivering a story.

Dramatize. Don't be afraid to ham it up a bit. Remember: you're trying to paint a picture. As you speak, focus on the scene in your mind and try to become part of it. Relive the story as you tell it.

Describe. Use a lot of details in the beginning of the story and then phase them out. Listeners need to hear more details while you're creating the context. A good rule of thumb is to start by using more details than you think the story needs. Your goal is to draw your listener into the scene. Once you establish the context and you move on to the challenge and climax, you need fewer details.

Shift. As you're telling the story, you sometimes act as a guide. Other times, you're part of the action. In other words, you step in and out of the scene. These dual functions make it acceptable for the storyteller to shift between the past tense and the present tense.

Pause. Timing is key to good storytelling. So-called 'pregnant pauses' can entice your protégé and imbue a story with drama and suspense. If you are not accustomed to telling stories, practice by recording your story on audiotape and listening for places where pauses might add punch. Then tell your story at a pace that is slow, but not too slow.

Gesture. Use different gestures, varied facial expressions, and dramatic body movements. Such techniques can help turn a written story into a living demonstration.

Stay focused. The proverbial admonition to 'stick to the story' is good advice. The storyteller who goes off on tangents loses momentum and ultimately frustrates listeners. Don't introduce secondary issues or new words and concepts. And don't ask questions during the story. Questions can be effective learning tools, but they tend to break the thread of the narrative.

Stay positive. Even sad stories should have an element of joy. Avoid biting sarcasm and satire. If a story is too acerbic, protégés tend to resist. The same goes for exaggeration. Most storytellers tend to embellish stories and tailor them to fit their needs and goals. That's expected, but too much poetic license can actually undermine the authenticity and realism that make a story powerful. If your protégé does not buy your story, she or he probably won't buy your learning points either.

Stories fit just about anywhere. As an introduction, a story can announce and organize the main points of the learning to follow. As a conclusion, a story can reiterate the core principles, ideas, and concepts of the mentoring session. Stories can act as breathers. They can provide welcome respites when topics are complex or abstract, and they can alleviate emotionally charged discussions.

Stories can engage learning emotionally and show protégés the consequences of taking or omitting certain actions. But it isn't enough simply to 'make up a story.' As with most worthwhile endeavors, effective storytelling requires thorough planning.

"You've got to sing like you don't need the money. You've got to love like you'll never get hurt. You've got to dance like there's nobody watching. You've got to come from the heart if you want it to work."
— Susanna Clark

CHAPTER 19
Passionate Connections
THE MENTOR'S GREATEST GIFT

Larry Smith lost it! And he lost it in — of all places — the big-deal quarterly executive meeting. He went absolutely over the edge in his impassioned plea on some issue concerning a customer. No, he wasn't angry — but he was intense. And although he demonstrated a few gestures that would be the envy of any aspiring thespian, he didn't pound the table.

But what Larry did, in his out-of-control passion, clearly crossed all normal bounds of rationality and routine boardroom decorum — and engaged the hearts and commitment of every person in the meeting. All were truly moved. People may be instructed by reason, but they are inspired by passion. It *did* make a difference. Stuff happened!

Larry Smith was the real-life vice president of service management for PKS Information Services in Omaha, Nebraska. The scene was a typical meeting at PKS, where rationality is routinely relegated to the sidelines and people, particularly senior officers, are encouraged to passionately connect with others on any issue, especially a customer issue. PKS is one of the winners in the information services outsourcing business. Just as there was David talk in Goliath Land after stones were thrown, PKS is no doubt regularly the subject of water cooler conversations at EDS, IBM, and other major competitors. And for good reason: The folks at PKS are tops at what they do.

The 'Larry loses his cool' incident at PKS led me to reflect on the true meaning of contemporary leadership and mentoring. I thought about how so much mainstream corporate culture is invested in control, consistency, and keeping one's cool. And I thought about how little these values had anything to do with the fervor, spirit, and passion with which people who love their work achieve success.

People don't brag about their rational marriages, their reasonable hobbies, or their sensible vacations. In-control behavior is nowhere to be seen when Junior is rounding third base. Even taciturn anglers have things to say when the cork goes under and the cane pole bends double. But somehow all that ardor becomes an unwelcome and embarrassing aberration within corporate walls. And the closer one gets to mahogany row, the less tolerance you find for sounds of the heart.

I also thought about how liberating it was for everyone in that room when Larry lost his cool. Were we uncomfortable? Yes! Did we wonder, where the hell is this going? Yes! But we all felt momentarily in touch with real life. It made me remember the poem about the moth fatally attracted to the flame but 'feeling more alive in that final moment than I have ever felt in my life.' Shelby Latcherie, Julia Roberts's character in the movie *Steel Magnolias*, echoed this sentiment when, as an expectant mother eager to give birth but facing potentially fatal complications from diabetes, she chose 'thirty minutes of wonderful' over a life-time of 'nothing special.'

Great mentors are not always rational beings; they are often flame seekers. They give passionate birth in the face of threatening circumstances. The biography of almost every great leader who ever faced the potential of bodily harm in pursuit of a cause communicates a consistent theme: *Why* we were there played so loud in my ear I never really heard *what* might happen *because* we were there. These leaders put issues such as personal safety and control on some emotional back burner and let passion lead. We know Larry; he's not an irrational, illogical person. Yet somehow we trusted his passion as much as his reason — perhaps more.

PASSION IS HONEST

Passion is more honest than reason. To be sure, logic is more elegant, more sensible, and surely more prudent. And one feels far safer and calmer with the rational; predictability never makes the heart race. Passion leaves us fearing an on-the-edge, unanticipated outcome. It also makes us feel free, alive, and somehow real and whole. And when leaders evoke that feeling in us, we are somehow more energized, more like a soldier ready for battle.

When I was an infantry unit commander in Vietnam, young men went into battle daily with no knowledge of the complex sociopolitical ramifications of the war. Yet these men were ready to die. For what? For duty, honor, and country. Can any cause be more illogical and amorphous? What's the sense of charging an entrenched sniper who will almost certainly add you to his body count? For duty? What's the rationale behind bleeding to death in a rice paddy far from Cincinnati or Cheyenne or Charlotte? Honor? What brought GIs from Alamo, Hoxie, and Sterling the silver star and the distinguished service cross? It was passion, not reason. Action was spurred by the spirit of the moment, not the logic of geopolitics.

What would you die for at work?

'Die for?' you ask. 'Are you insane?'

Consider this: Is not business welfare as important to our global survival as national pride?

'Whoa!' you may say. 'We can't survive the chaos of unbridled emotion and the confusion of out-of-control desire. What would the stockholders say? After all, is it not the role of our leaders to bring forth grace under pressure, to keep their cool when all around them are losing theirs? Should leaders not strive to be more anchor than sail? More rudder than oar?'

No! And again — No!

We have missed the boat on what it means to be a leader and a mentor. The world, the organization, and the situation offer far more predictability than is required. Leaders do not have to *add* order, sanity, rationality, or logic. Every seam of business life is stretched to bursting with those qualities. On the contrary, a truly sane leader, one faced with the daunting task of stirring the troops to action, fosters insane passion. A memorable leader calls up in each of us a visit to the ragged edge of brilliance and the out-of-the-way corner of genius.

When we feel inspired, incensed, ennobled, we have visited the magic realm of passion. Typically, we return from that realm renewed, revitalized — and perhaps a bit embarrassed at discovering our unsuspected talents. And when a leader has had a hand in showing us the way to that realm, we return with a new sense of partnership.

PASSION IS INVITATIONAL

"There is an energy field between humans," wrote *Love and Will* author and philosopher Rollo May, "and when a person reaches out in passion, it is usually met with an answering passion." Passionate connections invite passionate responses — and leadership and mentoring are fundamentally about invitation.

Ask twenty people to name the greatest leader of all time. Sure, you might get a general or two, but the list will probably have more leaders who stirred their followers with fire than leaders who motivated with reasoning. The names John Kennedy, Winston Churchill, Martin Luther King, Jr., Mother Teresa, and Albert Schweitzer are not connected so much with rationalism as with passion; nor are Bruce Nordstrom, Southwest Airlines' Herb Kelleher, or the late Sam Walton. The great leader's invitation to action is his own passion.

In his powerful book *Leading Change*, James O'Toole finds a strong case for passion in his study of a modern American industrial prophet. Why were Edwards Deming's concepts of quality so late to be embraced by his own country? Was it Yankee arrogance? Why did the Japanese embrace Deming and his views early, showing him an almost godlike reverence, while his own country treated him like a half-mad geezer?

Deming connected passionately with the Japanese people. O'Toole quotes the director of the Japanese Union of Scientists and Engineers: "[Deming] loved Japan and the Japanese from his own heart. The enthusiasm with which he did his best for his courses still lives and will live forever in the memory of all concerned. . . . Featuring all these educational activities was his deep love and high humanness." When he returned to the United States, he expressed not love but disdain for those who formerly had shunned his views. No Japanese ever described Deming as ornery or difficult to work with — yet most American executives found Deming's attitude toward them gruff, inflexible, sometimes callous. O'Toole hypothesizes that Deming's own demons may have been the greatest obstacle to getting his brilliant concepts of quality embraced in his homeland.

One of my partners, Ron Zemke, and I checked into a midtown New York hotel one evening. I approached a desk clerk with a mile-wide smile and a jovial disposition. Remembering my late mother-in-law's line, "A stranger is a friend you haven't met yet," I made twenty seconds of small talk with the desk clerk, calling him by his name, which I saw on his uniform jacket. My partner was at the tail end of head cold and had just gotten off an eight-hour flight. He was, to put it diplomatically, in a rather somber mood and had little to say to the desk clerk at his end of the counter.

Our plan was to go to our respective rooms, drop our luggage, and rendezvous in my room before dinner. And that's what we did. Ron dropped his luggage in his room, then came across the hall to my — suite!

"How did you get a suite?" he asked with obvious irritation.

"My Southern accent!" I replied.

The truth obviously lay in the fact that I took the time — a whole twenty seconds — to connect with my desk clerk. And what a difference it made: seventy-five square feet, Ron would say with mild bemusement. But the story doesn't end there. When we returned from dinner, my message light was on: My desk clerk had called to make sure my room was satisfactory. Ron's message light was not on. Passion is invitational.

PASSION IS A 'DASHBOARD SPECIAL'

When I was a teenager, one of my classmates, Charles Holland, worked part time at the Tastee Treat, the local after-school, after-movie, after-ballgame hangout. Charles invented a drink he called a 'Dashboard Special.' It had a base of 'co-cola' (as we referred to Coke® back then) to which he added a shot of every syrup he had in his soda fountain — chocolate, butterscotch, vanilla, cherry, everything. It was not very tasty, but it became the local symbol for daring and bold. When someone was 'feeling his oats,' he would say, "Gimme a Dashboard Special." It wasn't a macho thing, but a bold, 'go for it' move — a passionate option.

Whatever you may call the form it takes in your mentoring partnership — commitment, boldness, you name it — passion is magical! W. H. Murray, in his book *The Scottish Himalayan Expedition*, wrote: "Until one is committed, there is hesitancy, the chance to draw back, always ineffectiveness. The moment one definitely commits oneself, then Providence moves, too. All sorts of things occur to help one that would never otherwise have occurred." Goethe called it "boldness" and said, "Whatever you can do, or dream you can, begin in boldness. Boldness has genius, power, and magic in it." And philosopher Hegel wrote, "We may affirm absolutely that nothing great in the world has been accomplished without passion." Passion takes the plain vanilla out of encounters. It's a Dashboard Special leap into relationships.

Protégés, like all partners, need passionate connections. Leaders who lead from the heart awaken boldness in others. They build a relationship platform that raises everyone to a higher level. Confederate General Thomas J. Jackson was never again called 'Tom' after someone spotted him calmly directing defenses on the battlefield at Bull Run and remarked, "There stands General Jackson like a stone wall." His troops came to be known for the same spirited, never-say-die passion in combat. And who can forget the same phenomenon among leaders named Martin, Mahatma, and Susan B.? Reason instructs, but passion inspires.

> "One person with passion is better than forty people merely interested."
>
> — E. M. Forster

Why are you here on this earth, in this role, at this time? What difference will your being here make? What legacy will you leave behind? Will you be forgotten for what you maintained or remembered for what you contributed? Imposing mountains are climbed, culture-changing movements are started, and breakthrough miracles are sparked by leaders who transcended rationalism and prudence, letting their spirit soar from within. Order the Dashboard Special for Larry Smith — and have one yourself!

CHAPTER 20
For the Protégé
ACCEPTING GIFTS WITHOUT GUILT

When we left off from our last 'For the Protégé' section, Sage was saying to you . . .

"Let Dale know you're eager to get into the thick of the mentoring session. Dale needs your signal now."

"Dale, I'm feeling really excited about how this session is going. I'd like to throw out a problem I'm having and get your thoughts on how I might handle it."

Dale seems pleased with your enthusiasm to get things going. The two of you explore several ways that you might address the problem you're having. At one point Dale gives you pointed feedback, at another useful advice, and later, as the conversation nears its end, a poignant story about his own struggle with a situation similar to yours in which he eventually solved the problem in a way that would be very difficult for you to try.

You suddenly feel awkward, as though you don't belong in this conversation. You find yourself wanting concede to Dale's point . . . even though you don't entirely agree.

"Feeling guilty, aren't you!" Sage whispers in your ear when you least expect it. At least it is confirmation that your ears are working. You were beginning to wonder if that ringing was permanent.

"What Dale is doing for you is just as beneficial to Dale as it is to you. Sit up, look at Dale, and show your gratitude. You both have earned this moment. There is no debt to be paid here. Just benefits free for your use."

"Thank you for that, Dale. I need to think about it some more. You've given me a lot to chew on."

Dale takes your affirmation in stride and continues to offer a few more suggestions. However, this time his advice is interspersed with questions . . . as if he were poking through a minefield, using your reactions to the questions as guidance on where to step next.

You are beginning to feel as though you have carefully lassoed the conversation back from being a monologue, with you the sole spectator, to now being a dialogue with a valued partner.

Part V

Extending:
NURTURING A SELF-DIRECTED LEARNER

Extending

NURTURING A SELF-DIRECTED LEADER

> Conversation is but carving!
> Give no more to every guest
> Than he's able to digest.
> Give him always of the prime,
> And but little at a time.
> Carve to all but just enough,
> Let them neither starve nor stuff,
> And that you may have your due,
> Let your neighbor carve for you.
>
> — Jonathan Swift, "Conversation"

There are limits to dialogue. This book thus far has assumed that all mentoring occurs in a high-quality conversation between a mentor and a protégé. While it is true that the mentoring process is largely a conversational proceeding, it would be shortsighted and limiting to assume that dialogue is the only path to discovery and insight.

In fact, dialogue itself can be seductive, and the relationship can be codependent. Mentor and protégé in time become very comfortable with each other. The mentor derives personal satisfaction from watching the protégé learn; this leads to more conversation, more encounters. The protégé also finds pleasure in the wisdom of the mentor and the spirit of the consultation. While comfort is clearly helpful for communication, it can be a barrier to experimentation. Both mentor and protégé look forward to the next meeting, ultimately becoming so dependent on the relationship that neither is inclined to risk losing it.

While 'codependent' might seem too strong a word, even a small degree of dependency can spoil the spirit of growth. The litmus test is the emotional discomfort either party would experience if the relationship came to an end. If either party's need to end the relationship is marked by guilt or resistance, some codependency has probably infiltrated the relationship.

An effective way to avoid codependency is to extend the learning beyond dialogue. As new forms of learning become available, the protégé discovers new routes to self-sufficiency. The ultimate extension takes the mentor completely out of the equation, leaving the protégé to find his or her own way to competence — and independence.

The bias of most managers is to narrow, not extend, to build loyalty rather than liberty. Consequently, this final core competence is rather counterintuitive, much like surrendering, accepting, and gifting. However, as uncomfortable as it may be, the greatest contribution you can make to the protégé's development is to let the relationship evolve to a point at which you are no longer needed. That contribution begins with extending.

CHAPTER 21
Beyond the Relationship
ENSURING THE TRANSFERENCE OF LEARNING

There are many advantages to being raised on a farm. You learn a lot about how nature really works. Instead of watching milk come pouring out of a carton, you get to see it come squirting out of a cow.

On a farm, milk made its way to your glass the long way around. It was the product of the bribery of a bag of feed, special squeezes on a reluctant udder, numerous restarts after the milk pail was kicked over or a tail in pursuit of a fly was deposited inside, slow straining through cheese cloth, plus careful skimming and cooling. All the pictures in some citified textbook could not adequately tell the tale of milk making like a seat on a three-legged stool in a smelly barn with an impatient cow.

Mentoring can be an exhilarating but ineffective experience if mentors talk like a textbook and fail to offer a seat on the stool. Mentoring does not end with advice, feedback, and instruction. The goal of mentoring is not simply learning. The goal of mentoring is to foster betterment . . . better performance, greater productivity, higher effectiveness. Granted there is merit in learning for learning's sake. But in today's business world with its razor-thin margins, learning must be for result's sake. Mentors don't have the luxury of helping protégés increase their knowledge but not their use of that knowledge.

Transfer of learning has been the challenge for all learning facilitators — be they teachers, professors, trainers, or mentors. The argument often posited is, 'Once they leave my tutelage, it is up to them to put it to use.' That argument is usually punctuated with old saws about leading horses to water. Great mentors know, however, that the experiment isn't over until the learner has tried it out in the laboratory of life. And there are all sorts of actions that help ensure that what is learned in the relationship actually 'takes.'

LEND A HELPING HAND

Peter Senge wrote in *The Fifth Discipline*: "When we see that to learn, we must be willing to look foolish, to let another teach us, learning doesn't always look so good anymore . . . only with the support and fellowship of another can we face the dangers of learning meaningful things." The key word is fellowship — a word that combines the constitution of a partnership with the warmth of camaraderie.

Look for ways to 'be there' when your protégé has 'opening night.' Remember that rehearsal is always a far cry from the reality of actual performance. Boldness within the cloistered safety of a mentoring relationship is quite different from bravery in the school of hard knocks. When your protégé is slated to engage in her or his first attempt at 'flying solo,' send your well wishes and affirmation. Call after the fact to learn of the outcome. Regardless of the success or failure of the first time out, be supportive. Offer your help; do not automatically give your help. Your protégé needs to feel independent, not still saddled with a 'Father knows best' Monday morning quarterback.

If you can actually be there, assume the role of fan and cheerleader, not sideline coach. Let your protégé know you are there, feeling excited and confident. But avoid the grandstanding of the doting parent eagerly letting the stands know, 'That's my kid!'

Run appropriate interference to help ensure your protégé has a fair chance at putting his or her new learning into practice. This may entail securing support or permissions from others who may affect the protégé's performance. One of my early mentors supplemented our sessions by arranging for me to attend a two-day workshop with a renowned guru in the field. But he didn't stop there. When I returned enthusiastic and full of new ideas, I was surprised to get a call from the president of the company inviting me to lunch to discuss how I might implement what I had learned. His interest gave me courage to push the initial resistance of my colleagues. I learned a few years later that my mentor had suggested to the president that he give ear to my new learnings.

Be Vigilant for Obstacles to Learning

Consultant Geary Rummler says, "You can take highly motivated, well-trained employees, put them in a lousy system, and the system will win every time." Effective learning results can become ineffective performance results if the protégé enters a system, process, or unit that punishes — or simply does not encourage — the newly acquired skills. A crucial part of your role is to be ever vigilant for obstacles that undermine the learning acquired through your mentoring.

Think of your protégé's learning as a newly planted tree. In time the tree will have deep roots and a hardy resistance to wind, disease, and extreme temperatures. But, as a sapling, it is particularly vulnerable. It must be supported, protected, and meticulously cared for until it can fend for itself. So it is with a protégé. As a novice, new skills are still weak and unstable. Defending new behavior against external pressures to go back to the old way is challenging. Protégés need mentors to aid in their struggle to sustain new skills.

Several years ago I consulted with a large high-tech firm eager to make customer service its claim to fame. The CEO decided that everyone on the front line would be assigned a mentor to meet with weekly for an hour to talk about customer-service challenges. Managers were given mentoring training, procedures were put in place to ensure the weekly mentor-protégé meetings occurred, and everyone was happy with the initial results. In fact, customer service scores made significant jumps as front-line employees, armed with enhanced skills and newfound support, turned indifference into enthusiasm.

Six months into the mentoring project, the CEO decided to delegate the system-wide effort to someone in a staff role. It signaled a dampening of commitment. Managers were pressured to trim their one-hour sessions to thirty minutes; then weekly became monthly. As results declined and customer satisfaction scores turned downward, pressure was put on the staff leader to 'fix it.' The solution was to take an iron fist approach to paperwork completion. Early enthusiasm turned to cynicism and resentment. The company was acquired, the CEO replaced, and the mentoring endeavor was replaced with more hard-line, cost-cutting efforts. You can imagine how the rest of the story played out.

BE AN ADVOCATE FOR INFORMAL LEARNING

Being a great mentor includes fostering an environment that values and nurtures learning. This means advocating informal learning. And there are a myriad of ways to make learning a natural part of the work world.

A major consulting firm found that professional reading among employees increased when the firm installed magazine racks with professional journals in the lavatories. The firm's president discovered that surprisingly few journals were absent-mindedly removed, and employees began contributing their own copies of journals to which the firm did not subscribe. Comments like 'Did you read that article about . . .?' were frequently interjected in staff meetings, which further reinforced the amount of informal learning through journal reading.

> "Learn as though you would never be able to master it; hold it as though you would be in fear of losing it."
> — Confucius, 6th Century

Company magazines, newsletters, and bulletin boards can also be a good source of learning for employees. An insurance company found the most popular articles in its company magazine were interviews with executives, managers, and employees dealing with what their area was engaged in at the time. Done with clever layout and graphics, 'to all employees' media can serve as a valuable but inexpensive way of fostering employee learning. The unit or company intranet can likewise be a great boon to learning.

Another approach to informal learning is cross-unit sharing. A large research and development company effectively employed this process. Once a month a work group met for breakfast with a group from a different part of the company. Each unit would take thirty minutes to describe their function and current projects. The remaining thirty minutes was devoted to informal conversation among the work groups in a cocktail party fashion. The company found the monthly hour-and-a-half breakfast gathering an effective way of increasing employee breadth and decreasing inter-unit conflict. A bank used a similar arrangement but added a tour of the respective work areas to the cross-unit sharing process. Allotting staff meeting time for people to report on what was learned at a major conference or following the completion of a workshop or course signals that learning is valued.

Learning that ends when the protégé bids adieu to the mentor is likely retained only until the protégé reaches the elevator. Given the shaky tentativeness of new learning, it is up to the mentor to come up with ways to help shelter, support, and nurture it until it 'takes.' Knowing how to eliminate barriers and erect supports to buttress the learner until habits are cemented and competencies are hardwired can go a long way to help the learning-transfer process for your protégé. Most important is to create a climate that prizes not only ongoing learning but also risk taking in the protégé's trying out new knowledge and skills back on the job.

CHAPTER 22
Managing Sweet Sorrow

LIFE AFTER MENTORING

Effective mentoring relationships are rich, engaging, and intimate. But all such arrangements must come to an end, and no matter how hard we may try to avoid it, every ending has a bittersweet dimension. As Shakespeare so eloquently reminds us, "Parting is such sweet sorrow." As you and your protégé reach the end of your partnership, how do you manage 'farewell' with a focus on 'well'?

GOING FOR GROWTH

You would be remiss in your duties as a mentor to make the parting an occasion for lingering regret. Healthy mentoring relationships use separation as a tool for growth. Below are several ideas for ending a mentoring relationship gracefully and constructively.

Celebrate with Fanfare and Stories

Celebration need not be a party with band and banner; it can be as simple as a special meal together, a drink after work, a peaceful walk in a nearby park. The point of celebration, however, is to mark the end of the mentoring relationship. Celebration is a rite of passage, a powerful symbol of closure and of moving on to the next learning plateau.

In a workshop I conducted for a well-known West Coast software manufacturer, a manager mentioned that he was getting reports from other managers that supervisors who transferred from his department seemed to take longer than usual to adjust to their new supervisory roles. It was beginning to hurt his reputation within the organization as a supplier of competent talent. I asked him to play back in reverse the events leading from his supervision to their new roles. It quickly became clear that their relationships with him never came to a formal end — they simply stopped. Later, when he began including the ritual of a celebrative closure on their last day under his supervision, the adjustment problems vanished.

Celebration should be rich in compliments and stories, laughter and joy. Your protégé graduate needs your blessing more than your brilliance; your good wishes more than your warnings. Avoid the temptation to lay on one last caution. Your kindest contribution will be a solid sendoff with gifts of confidence, compassion, and consideration.

Solidify Learning with Nostalgia

When I left Bank of America (then NCNB) in 1979 to form a management consulting firm, Chuck Cooley, my boss and mentor of eight years, treated me to breakfast at a nearby site he and I had used countless times for mentoring meetings. He asked me two questions, both important to our parting and my growth: 'Whom would I recommend as my successor, and why?' and 'What were the primary lessons I had learned over the eight years?' His second question was his gentle way of getting me to reflect on how far I had come: from a green assistant training director to a seasoned director of management and organization development. Not willing to rely solely on my memory, he repeatedly interjected 'Remember the time when . . .?' stories. My departure was peaceful and complete.

> "Communicate unto the other person that which
> you would want him to communicate unto you
> if your positions were reversed."
> — Aaron Goldman

Lace your final meetings with opportunities to remember, reflect, and refocus. Let your recall questions bridge the discussion toward the future; merely reminiscing can mire the meeting in melancholy. Listen to your protégé with the devotion you would give your mentor. Honor your mature protégé with respect and recognition. After my last meeting with Chuck I stood taller than at my college graduation. He paid me homage by honoring my development.

Let Time Pass before Follow-Up

The quickest route to delivering a message of dependence is to follow up with a protégé too soon after departure. Wait a week or more before calling or visiting. Setting your relationship free takes space and time. Should you follow up at all? Absolutely! Partners follow up on partners. The key is, not too quickly. Allow weaning time.

Let your protégé be his or her own person. There may be times when a former protégé is being honored and you will feel the urge to share the limelight. I once had a professor who always wanted to share the credit when one of his students achieved some award. While pride was obviously a part of his response — 'I was his major professor' — the action tended to keep his former protégé stuck in the 'I'm still his student' position. Let go. Move on. Celebrate the past but concentrate on the future.

Just as rapport building is crucial to the beginning of a mentoring relationship, a sense of adjournment is equally important at its end. Letting go is rarely comfortable, but it's necessary if the protégé is to flourish and continue to grow out of the mentor's shadow. In the final analysis, the upper limit of growing is 'grown,' implying closure and culmination. Mark the moment by managing adjournment as a visible expression of achievement and happiness.

CHAPTER 23

The Kaizen of Mentoring

LEARNING, LEARNING, LEARNING

H e that's not busy being born is busy dying," sang folk singer Bob Dylan in the mid-sixties. His observation is still relevant. In today's world of enterprise, 'being born' is about growth and 'dying' is about obsolescence, reduced productivity, and unemployment. And the word most applicable to mentoring today is 'busy.' Learning never stops.

As they help their protégés grow, good mentors work on their own growth. They don't grow simply to be role models for protégés; they grow to enhance their own worth. Mentors most adept at self-mentoring are those who choose a wide range of avenues for learning. This chapter is dedicated to the self-mentoring needs of mentors.

INSIDE . . .

The famous Dr. Seuss children's rhyme "inside, outside, upside down" suggests a route to personal growth. Learning can be thought of as coming from three different directions. Directed growth begins with a close personal examination — a look *inside* that includes a thoughtful examination of strengths, limitations, improvement opportunities, needs, hopes, and fears. Ask yourself questions like those suggested by Gary Heil, Tom Parker, and Rick Tate in their book *Leadership and the Customer Revolution:*

- What major area have I changed my mind about in the last quarter?

- How long has it been since my assumptions about something important were absolutely dead wrong?

- When I compare the way I think this year with the way I thought last year, what is different?

- What have I learned this quarter that makes my actions last quarter seem less effective?

- Is there someone I am close to who thinks very differently than I do, and what have I learned from that person?

- How much time have I spent in the last quarter seriously questioning the way I think?

- What was the last skill I learned with my associates? From my associates? From my protégé?

- How long has it been since I lost an important argument with one of my associates?

... OUTSIDE ...

After you've taken a look inside, your next step is to consider *outside* resources. Where are your learning opportunities likely to be richest? Most accessible? What people, tools, supports, and permissions might you need for effective learning? What resources are going to be important to your growth? Are there resources you can borrow, trade for, buy, or get simply for the asking? Leave no stone unturned.

There is an old joke about a man who tried to escape a rising flood by climbing to the roof of his house. Rescuers came by in a boat and pleaded with the man to come with them and escape the flood. "No," said the man, "I have put my faith in the Almighty. I will be fine." An hour later another boat came by to save the man, now on the highest point of his roof as the floodwaters continued to rise. Again he refused rescue. Some time later a helicopter flew over his house and the crew tried to persuade the man, now sitting on top of his chimney, to climb the rope ladder and escape. Again the man said, "No, I have put my faith in the Almighty. Go away, I will be fine."

> "Only the curious will learn and only the resolute overcome the obstacles to learning. The quest quotient has always excited me more than the intelligence quotient."
> — Eugene S. Wilson

The man drowned. Soon he found himself at the Pearly Gates. Angrily, he confronted St. Peter: "How could you let me down? I put my faith in the Almighty and you did nothing to save me!"

St. Peter looked at his clipboard and with great puzzlement responded, "I don't understand it either. According to this, we sent you two boats and a helicopter!"

. . . UPSIDE DOWN

There are many resources available for our growth. Some, however, are well disguised, requiring us to look in out-of-the-way places, turn things *upside down*, and squint to find them. What are your greatest strengths? What components of those strengths have liabilities? I have a colleague who is an excellent editor. However, this asset keeps him from writing articles he could and should write. "The critical parent in my head seems to keep me from ever completing the first paragraph," he admits. What is the least appealing route to growth that you might pursue? What aspects of that might be beneficial to you? What insight might you gain from enlisting a personal coach? What might you learn about yourself through mentoring a child not related to you? Do you have any weird or avant-garde friends who might expose you to new perspectives?

LITTER YOUR NEST WITH NUTS

When we had our trees trimmed, some large oak limbs contained old squirrel nests. Every nest that came tumbling to the ground revealed that the squirrels had not just stored nuts in the ground nearby, they had plenty in their nest. Learning needs the same storage system. Avoid the 'out of sight, out of mind' trap by littering the world in which you live with opportunities to learn.

Is there a magazine rack in your bathroom at home? Do you have tapes in your car on a subject important to your growth? Have you used your library card in the last six months? Are there magazines you would read more often if you had a subscription? Is there always a book in progress in your briefcase or flight bag? Put a pad, pencil, and pen light beside your bed so ideas that visit you at 2:00 a.m. are not lost by dawn. Trade in watching television for a hobby that expands your mind. Trash the computer games on your laptop. Read! Write! Think!

START A LEARNING JOURNAL

Journalizing has proven to be a powerful tool for personal growth. Just as a Day-Timer® helps in priority management and organization, a journal gently forces us to be disciplined, focused, and reflective. Like a counselor or therapist, a journal helps us transform information into understanding. As a synthesizing device, a journal extends our learning beyond predictable skills to deeper awareness and mastery.

There are countless ways to keep a journal. Go to the bookstore or office supply store and purchase a bound, blank book to capture your journal entries. Every day — preferably at about the same time — jot down your thoughts about what you have learned, your reaction to the learning, and your plans for using it. Journals are records for review. Once a week, review your daily entries; every month, review the previous four weeks. Coach yourself to dig deep as you analyze and assess. Note themes, patterns, and trends. Pretend you are reviewing the journal of someone you do not know. What advice would you offer? What cautions might you urge? What suggestions?

READ BOOKS

Writers recommend books. Surprise, surprise! Even as I list some of my favorite books, I will echo a criticism a colleague leveled at me early in my career: "Chip, you read too much and don't think enough." He was on the mark. Some of my motivation to read books was not about learning but about boasting. As you read, periodically stop and ask: 'What can I do with what I am learning? What are the larger, grander, deeper implications of what this book is telling me?'

A word of caution about my list: Different books speak to people in different ways and at different times in their careers. Whatever book you select for whatever purpose, carefully read the preface, scan the content cover to cover, read a fourth of the book. If you're not drawn in, select another. If you believe you've given a book a fair chance to teach you but you're not getting a return on time invested, don't waste another minute on it.

My list of favorite books below was assembled with one purpose in mind: to help you become the best mentor you can be. Some of the books are new; some are old, worthy of a second reading.

My favorite coaching book is *Coaching Knock Your Socks Off Service*, by my partner Ron Zemke. Another is *Coaching for Leadership: How the World's Greatest Coaches Help Leaders Learn*, edited by Marshall Goldsmith, Laurence Lyons, and Alyssa Freas.

I still enjoy rereading *Zen and the Art of Motorcycle Maintenance*, by Robert Pirsig; popular a few years back, it taught me a lot about following the flow of relationships rather than driving them to my own ends. Max DePree's *Leadership Jazz* offers a clear, pragmatic look at the leader as partner. I am also a fan of the work of John Gardner, particularly *On Excellence*.

Peter Vaill's *Spirited Leading and Learning* offers refreshing insights into the role of spirit in relationships. Jerry Harvey's *Abilene Paradox* has always helped me get past some of the absurdity of organizational life. Finally, I would recommend that you reread *The Little Prince*, by Antoine Saint-Exupéry; this childhood book contains surprisingly deep insights into the soul of mentoring.

CHAPTER 24
For the Protégé

GROWING UP MEANS STEPPING OUT

Where we left off from our last 'For the Protégé' . . .

Dale takes your affirmation in stride and continues to offer a few more suggestions. However, this time his advice is interspersed with questions . . . as if he were poking through a minefield, using your reactions to the questions as guidance on where to step next.

You are beginning to feel as though you have carefully lassoed the conversation back from being a monologue, with you the sole spectator, to now being a dialogue with a valued partner.

"I'm still not clear on what I should do next . . . ," you hear yourself saying to Dale. As the words leave your lips, you are uncomfortably aware that the two of you have just spent the last ten minutes laboriously outlining next steps.

"It's okay to be a little anxious about jumping into deep water by yourself. You'll do just fine. And remember, Dale is not expecting you to be perfect . . . just do your best."

"Let me restate that . . . ," you say in an obvious attempt to not look stupid. **"We covered next steps . . . I suppose I'm just a bit apprehensive about soloing on this one."**

Dale gives you that comforting 'I've been there myself' smile. You both laugh. Dale tells you quickly that you know what to do and how to do it . . . it is the 'trust yourself' kick in the pants you need. You set up your next mentoring session for next week. Dale promises to touch base with you in a day or so. You shake hands and exit his cubicle.

"You'll be great," you hear Sage softly speaking in your ear as you walk down the hallway. You are starting to enjoy the company of your own private mentor!

Part VI

Special Conditions

Special Conditions

Mentoring is rarely the simple, cooperative experience the Jack and Tracy story has demonstrated and the 'For the Protégé' chapters outlined. Mentoring often carries special challenges that test the skill of the mentor and try the patience of the protégé. Consider this section a special overlay for everything thus far covered in the book.

Two special conditions particularly affect the quality of the mentoring relationship: the players and the playground! In the chapter on unholy alliances we will explore several peculiar player conditions: peer-to-peer mentoring, mentoring a person at a higher position, and mentoring a person who is sufficiently 'different' to cause either of you anxiety. The most common differences are those at the core of most organizations' quest for diversity — gender, race/ethnicity, or creed. In our discussion, 'creed' will be used to cover a host of differences . . . an extreme conservative mentoring an extreme liberal, people of different sexual orientations, or a New York urbanite mentoring a South Georgia ruralite.

The core issue in unholy alliances is the fact that they *may* (not will) raise anxiety or apprehension in the mentor or protégé. When a special condition is discovered or acknowledged (it may be obvious), it is up to the mentor to raise the issue and attempt to gauge whether it is a source of anxiety. How that surfacing occurs can strongly influence the level of candor likely to used in the joint exploration.

The second type of special condition concerns the playground — the setting or context in which the mentoring relationship happens. Three conditions will be dissected: mentoring in a fast-paced world, mentoring when mentor and protégé are in different locations, and mentoring with the support or assistance of a non-human tool or resource. The first two — called white water mentoring and remote mentoring — are hallmarks of the contemporary work world. The third — using artificial intelligence — is by no means commonplace. However, with the advances being made in artificial intelligence (think R2D2 in *Star Wars* or Hal in *2001: A Space Odyssey*) and voice recognition technology, it is vital to prepare for their potential as a resource in mentoring.

CHAPTER 25
Unholy Alliances
MENTORING IN PRECARIOUS RELATIONSHIPS

A vis Bell was the toughest teacher I ever had. Her classroom standards for proper decorum were conspicuously stricter for me than any other student. Even my friends, who found Mrs. Bell a fun loving instructor more apt to charm than control, noticed the short leash she kept on me. She was dead set on never leaving the slightest perception that I was getting any hint of favoritism. Ninth grade was hard enough. But it was especially tough when your general science teacher was also your mother!

Mentoring is often about two relatively similar people — a wiser mentor and an eager-to-learn protégé — brought together for the facilitation of growth. However, that endeavor takes on a graver tone when the interpersonal relationship between mentor and protégé is dramatically outside the norm. Unholy alliances put a special pressure on the mentor. They likewise place unusual anxiety on the protégé.

The chances that a protégé would be the offspring of a mentor in today's world of enterprise are rare, if not unlikely. The example of my relationship with my teacher-mother is only symbolic of the diversity found in today's workplaces. However, it does figuratively telegraph the existence of many varieties of precarious relationships that can challenge the partnering aim of mentoring.

TRADING POWER FOR RESPECT: WHEN PUPILS ARE PEERS

When my son was a fourth-grader, he came home one day and announced that he had a new teacher assistant.

"Did your old teacher assistant leave?" I asked.

"No," he replied, "Mrs. Greer is still there."

"What's your new teacher assistant's name?" I asked.

Without looking up from kicking his soccer ball, he responded matter-of-factly: "Tommy."

I instantly knew this was weird. Fourth-graders don't refer to their teachers by their first names. Tenth-graders use teachers' first names as an act of rebellion;

twelfth-graders do it to sound grown up and cool. But most fourth-graders are not interested in being rebellious or cool.

As it turned out, Tommy was a sixth-grader and a part of a cross-age education effort to let older students tutor younger students. The concept was that elementary students often respond better to older peers than to a teacher, and placing teaching responsibility on the older students increased their growth as well.

Four months into my son's experience, I asked how he and Tommy were doing. "He's not a helper any more," he replied. I decided to keep my mouth closed to see if he would fill me in. He continued, "Tommy thought he knew more about math than me. And when I started getting answers faster than he did, he got really mad. He started calling me names. Mrs. Greer heard him and took his job away from him."

Peer mentoring poses special challenges no matter what the setting. Resistance is always an obstacle in mentoring, and it becomes especially acute when the mentor and protégé are peers. Most peer-mentors are painfully aware of how labels like 'smart aleck' and 'know-it-all' stick to those who profess to have wisdom they want to share. How do you make peer mentoring work when resistance so easily raises its ugly head? Hold that question while we consider another challenging situation.

MENTORING THE BOSS

How do you mentor someone in a higher position? The most common answer you will hear to that question is, 'Very carefully!'

As we have explored throughout this book, risk taking is tantamount to growth, and mixing learning and power produces a concoction that is typically risk-averse. This mixture is particularly powerful when mentoring a person in a higher position. Yet more and more organizations are, for example, asking younger employees who hold lower positions in the organization but possess key skills to be mentors to leaders in higher positions who need those skills. Consider, for example, the computer-illiterate CEO who asks the whiz-bang computer nerd in the bowels of the IT department, 'Come up to the penthouse suite and teach me how to use this thing!'

Mentoring the boss can carry another unfortunate by-product. The protégé can quickly become the brunt of employee resentment if seen as the 'teacher's pet.' Perceived favoritism can play havoc with an employee's position in an important peer group.

The general manager of a major New York hotel came from a section of that city not famous for interpersonal diplomacy. Wanting to soften her rather clipped, abrupt style, she sought the assistance of a charming front-desk supervisor. "The supervisor was thrilled I asked for her assistance," reported the GM. "But I could immediately sense some hesitation. After a bit of probing, I realized she was worried about being seen as someone trying to curry the favor of the boss. When I had asked her! So, at the next staff meeting I quelled her anxiety by announcing that I had insisted she be my mentor. "And," I told the staff, "after trying to turn me down, she relented and agreed to help me out." By adding a humorous touch to the announcement, I allayed any perception others might have that she might have been 'brownnosing the boss.'

How do you mentor someone in a higher position? Again, hold that question as we raise our final challenging situation.

MIXING MENTORING WITH DIVERSITY

My very first experience of being mentored by someone very different from me happened when I was five years old. It was a wonderful day in the life of my family: My parents proudly brought my baby brother, Jack, home from the hospital. Since the hospital was many miles away, they had been gone for several days.

I did not fully understand why their 'coming home' attention formerly aimed solely at my sister and me was now directed to this new addition. Instead of the usual 'we're home' toys that accompanied my parents' return from a trip, we got the 'special privilege' of coming (quietly) to look at a sleeping infant in a bassinet. This was a significant, happy time for my parents and yet I felt ignored, totally disenfranchised, and, at the same time, guilty for even having such feelings. I retreated to the base of a large pine tree out behind the garage to suffer alone.

I had not been out there very long when our wonderful African-American maid named Dee noticed my absence and interrupted my self-pity. Without speaking, she sat down on the ground beside me. Except for my muffled sniffles, we sat in silence for a long time. Then she began to tell me what it had been like to be a little girl in a family struggling in poverty. She spoke of a lifetime of harsh economics and trying tribulations. Then she smiled and talked about how lucky she felt to have grown to be a part of our family.

She described how being a part of our family brought with it the special opportunity of getting to know and love me. "And," she said, "just like me, you are going to get something very special. You are going to get to be the 'big brother' of that tiny baby in the house!" Then, she hugged me and left me alone to reflect on her words. I remember sitting for a long time. Then I went inside to look again at the infant I now privately pledged to protect.

Mentoring across differences — racial, ethnic, cultural, you name it — can be an exciting experience for mentor and protégé alike. No other relationship, done properly, poses such promise for reciprocal learning. No other relationship carries the such potential for growth. While our similarities offer us comfort, it is our differences that give us progress. And our dissimilarities enable us to discover the true essence of partnership: the realization that below our obvious differences lies a river we travel together. Dee's influence came through reaching across our differences to touch the part of our experience we shared. I felt isolated . . . so had she. I felt alone . . . so had she. But she had discovered a special gift in her new family. And she was there to help me discover I had just been given the exact same gift.

Humility First

Mentoring in challenging situations — with peers, people above, people who are different — requires an attitude of awe. Communicating that sense of wonderment is best done through an expression of raw, unedited humility. Humility is a special gift of managers who succeed as mentors. It is more than a gift in the case of peer, boss, and diversity mentoring — it's the key to the front door. If you start off by showing off your expertise, you're guaranteed to lose your non-captive audience. When a boss is doing the mentoring, protégés think they have to listen, and perhaps even act interested — but peers will simply blow you off and not waste their time. Bosses in the protégé position know they rank above you — and have the right to not be engaged.

> "Humility leads to strength and not to weakness. It is the highest form of self-respect."
> — John McCloy

With anyone who is 'different,' humility turns fear into connection — but humility is not a synonym for apology. To be humble means to be unassuming and egoless, acting from the soul without adding anything. You can be both humble and confident.

Ask Lots of Questions Up Front

Most protégés, when confronted with a mentor who does not fit the traditional mentor-protégé mold, show resistance at first: 'What the heck could you teach me?' 'Who appointed you Mister Know-It-All?' or 'I'm just a good as you!' Just like mentors, protégés sometimes harbor the notion that mentors should be superior. Any deviation from the traditional order of things makes them nervous. A crucial first step is to allay protégé anxieties and deal with the resistance.

One way to deal with resistance is to put enormous focus, energy, and attention on the protégé at the start of the relationship. Demonstrate dramatic listening. Forget about reciprocity for a while. Let the interest be one-sided — yours in the protégé. You'll get your turn later. Think of it this way: Every time you ask a question of the protégé, you gain a point. Every time you make a statement, you lose a point. And every time you make a statement about your background, your interest, your experience, or your anything, you lose five points. Get as many points as you can in the first ten minutes of the encounter.

Avoid Conditional Affirmations

My first job fresh out of college was as a management trainee in a large New Mexico bank. I started my one-year rotational training program as a teller in a small branch. After mastering the complexities of being a paying-and-receiving teller in a little over a month, I became the teller who balanced first at the end of each day — *the* sign of expertise. The branch manager, wanting to reward my accomplishment, assigned me to train a new teller, a Mexican-American twenty years my senior, who had come from another bank — and also a woman who had used up her lifetime supply of smiles in the job interview.

Armed with a new college degree and thirty-four days' experience, I thought I was hot stuff! But my freshman attempt at mentoring came to a screeching halt when I placed a loud 'but' at the end of a compliment about her work. She rose to her feet and coldly looked me over from head to toe. "Young man, you can never boss me! I was bossing when you were a gleam in your father's eye." With that announcement, she marched into the branch manager's office and demanded a transfer to another branch. I never dreamed that a single word — 'but' — could so powerfully render an effort ineffective.

Conditional affirmation ('Patsy, you're doing a great job, but . . .') has the effect of erasing the affirmation in the mind of the protégé. Also, because the critique now sounds parental, power and status issues are raised. So what do you do? Separate praise and criticism. If your goal is to praise, praise. If your goal is to criticize, criticize. Mixing the two in the same sentence or session can turn a confirming pat on the back into a controlling kick in the pants — especially when your protégé is your peer, your superior, or noticeably different from you.

Never Resist Resistance

One of the greatest lessons students of judo learn is never to resist resistance; instead, they learn to divert the energy of resistance to other uses. When you meet resistance with resistance, the barriers become more rigid, the heels of opposition dig deeper into the ground of power, and growth comes to a screeching halt.

Judo teaches students to use their opponent's energy by joining it and guiding it to a new place. Similarly, in a mentoring situation, you will do better to accept the learner's resistance and seek to learn from it. Pursue it, solicit it, and get it into the light of day by showing no fear of it. Treat conflict as a neutral force that can be applied to learning. Accept it as unresolved tension that needs to be understood to be channeled in a positive direction.

Strive for Reciprocal Learning

Pursue equality in your relationship. Learning happens best when it occurs on a level playing field. If your protégé sees you as a fellow learner (rather than as an 'I'll show you' smarty pants), there is greater potential for a partnership. With partnership comes acceptance, joint contribution, and growth.

Seek something your protégé knows that you would like to learn, and couple your mentoring with being a protégé to your protégé. Better still, pursue an area in which you both want to learn. One of my partners, Ron Zemke, has been an important mentor of mine for over twenty-five years; we've been business partners for over fifteen. He makes mentoring me a personal joy because he is just as interested in my mentoring him. As I get to be the student, I also get to be the teacher. The reciprocity is rarely a perfectly balanced fifty-fifty. Healthy relationships in all areas of life are sixty-forty one week and forty-sixty the next. Over time, however, the give-and-take clearly reflects a fair balance.

Mentoring in precarious relationships offers both special rewards and special challenges. The secret to success lies in taking what is ostensibly a unique relationship and managing the exchange of wisdom so that it maintains and honors equality. Focusing on humility, sincere consideration, authentic affirmation, and balance can foster an exchange that brings significant growth to both mentor and protégé.

CHAPTER 26
Arduous Alliances
MENTORING IN PRECARIOUS SITUATIONS

There are many learning alliances that are potentially arduous because of the precarious context in which the relationship is cast. We will examine three situations: mentoring in a super-fast-paced milieu, mentoring when the protégé is in a different location, and mentoring when technology (particularly artificial intelligence) is a part of the mentor-protégé mix. We will first examine white water mentoring.

MENTORING ON THE RUN: WHITE WATER WISDOM

Speed is both the genie and the ogre for today's supervisors. Some thrive on it; some long for the olden days. Like it or not, however, warp speed (a.k.a. cycle time, just-in-time, or out-of-time) is a trademark of our unpredictable work environments.

Dubbed 'permanent white water' by Peter Vaill in *Managing As a Performing Art*, the nature of today's business world challenges the supervisor's coaching and mentoring responsibilities. There are too many 'I'll have to get back to you' responses to 'Help me figure out how to' requests. The pressure to do wins out over the requirement to teach and learn. What can you do to coach on the run and still be effective? How can you keep up with the demands of the 'Time's up!' moment while making sure protégés receive the one-on-one attention, support, and tutelage they need to avoid skill obsolescence? Below are three tips for navigating through the white water.

Take Time for Learner Readiness

Great athletes always warm up, no matter how short the event. Under time pressure, many mentors tend to give short shrift to ascertaining whether the protégé is ready to learn. Lines like 'Let me get right to the punch line' risk neglecting the protégé's learning needs and leaving him overwhelmed and confused. Remember the old truism that longer planning time results in shorter implementation time, and less time overall? The same is true for learning.

No matter how little time you have for teaching, always take time to find out:

1. The employee's immediate learning needs and goals (What do you need to learn?),

2. Any pressing concerns that might affect how you would help, and

3. The employee's ideas on how you might be most helpful.

Beware of 'Let Me Just Show You How!'

Good mentors don't rescue, they support. The temptation of most leaders under the gun is to resort to demonstration rather than supportive direction. The real motivation behind 'Let me just show you how' is to get the work out while ostensibly helping the employee learn. This approach may boost short-term performance, but long-term proficiency suffers.

Does this mean that the mentor should never demonstrate a procedure? Of course not. The employee can often benefit from being shown how as she learns to do it for herself. But before you touch the keyboard, equipment, or report, ask yourself two questions:

1. Am I rescuing myself or supporting her? and

2. Will my demonstration increase or decrease independence?

Build Strong Parts Rather Than Weak Wholes

You're ten minutes away from rushing out the door to go to an important all-day meeting. One of your employees walks into your cubicle and announces, 'I'm stuck on this new M60 filterator process you asked me to learn. Can you spare a few minutes to help me figure it out?' You know that it will actually take thirty or forty minutes to explain adequately; the employee has received only an overview orientation. Being late to the meeting is not an option, but you want some M60 performance from this protégé today. What do you do?

Many mentors would give a ten-minute condensation of the forty-minute lesson and hope the employee could then muddle though. The result of such a hit-

and-run approach is likely to be complete confusion; an hour after you're gone, the employee will remember only a blur. A better approach is to identify the ten-minute part of your forty-minute lesson that is most crucial to getting started and cover that part thoroughly. Solid learning on a key part will create confident momentum and enable the protégé to learn the rest on his own. Competence in a limited area is better than vague awareness of the whole.

The futurists tell us that the days of 'Take your time!' are over for the business world; a 'Time's up!' pace, whether blessing or curse, is now essential to success. At the same time, employees must remain up to date on mastery of new skills. Superior mentors will be those who can competently tutor on the run.

MENTORING LONG DISTANCE: REMOTE LEARNING

I sat in the back row of a large, dimly lit auditorium filled with managers from a software company being treated to the last million-slide presentation of the day. Earlier I had spoken to this audience about the myths, merits, and methods of mentoring. A bright young systems engineer manager sitting three people to my right passed me a napkin with a handwritten note: "Do you have any suggestions on how I can mentor my people in Guam, Paris, and San Juan? They feel ignored and I feel guilty."

With only seventeen slides, polite applause, and the speaker's closing remarks to go, I had a little time to think. I can't remember now much about what I said — she seemed satisfied — but I can remember being struck by the realization that this dilemma is now commonplace.

We live in an era of self-directed work. Widening spans of control, downsizing, and rising numbers of employees without direct supervision have compelled leaders to supervise more and more at arm's length. Weak bosses feel relieved, their subordinates freed; but strong leaders can feel guilty and their subordinates ignored. The systems engineer's dilemma is becoming familiar to more and more leaders: How do you mentor when you're not there, and won't be for a while? How do you mentor long distance?

Create a Buddy System on Site

When you're not there, you're not there. It's important, therefore, to shore up other avenues for growth. A too-often-overlooked resource is the wisdom of peers. This doesn't mean going back to the old 'Watch Nellie' style of yesteryear. A true buddy system carefully matches protégé learning needs with the best colleague wisdom. To be effective, the buddy system must be based not just on availability but on purposeful matchmaking: personality matching, skill matching, and priority matching.

So how do I get Jane to mentor John on the Tillich technique when Jane and John are peers? First, hold Jane accountable for being supportive and available to mentor. Second, hold John accountable for seeking out Jane and learning the Tillich technique. Be sure to praise Jane for her mentoring, John for learning Tillich.

Easier said than done? Of course; isn't it always? Buddy systems work when we spend the effort to make them work. They require resources — especially time. Telling Jane to mentor John is great, but not if you don't cut Jane enough slack in her other duties.

Provide Learning Care Packages

I was working with a major hotel chain, teaching a part of their weeklong Lodging Leadership program. The participants were largely general managers from hotels around the world. It was lunchtime mid-week, and Steve, one of the program participants from a large hotel in New Orleans, received a large package. Many people gathered around as Steve opened the surprise. The package was filled with an assortment of items: a coffee mug, a favorite candy bar, various snacks, a package of pencils, a note pad, an inexpensive pair of reading glasses, sleeping pills, playing cards. It was from all the employees in his hotel back home. He was visibly moved. The practicality of the items was irrelevant; he had been remembered — and valued! He was instantly reminded of his commitment to do his best for his people.

Part of mentoring long distance is letting the protégé experience your concern and caring in tangible ways. An article, CD-ROM, or book on a topic of interest or need, a special job aid, or an audiotape on a work-related topic can send a powerful message that the person is remembered — and valued! Give the protégé a subscription to a magazine important to his professional growth. Place him on the routing list for growth-oriented items coming from your office.

When you are on site with the protégé, make note of small items he may not have but would find useful. Stationery and supplies may be stockroom items that can be had for the asking; unique items may take a bit more thought and planning. Could he use a rubber stamp of his business address? Is there a user list to which you could helpfully add his name? How would the protégé react to getting a package of post-it notes with his name printed on them? Care packages are limited only by your imagination; the best are those tailored to the protégé's individual needs, preferences, and situation.

Find Surrogate Mentors

When you can't be there in person, send an agent on your behalf. How many old B-grade war movies have you watched in which the hard-nosed general shows a surprising soft side by sending a valued expert in to assist? 'The General asked me to drop by and see if I might be able to lend a hand!' It was usually a turning point in the movie. Learning agents are allies of growth; they can fill a gap, shore up a weakness, or simply lend confidence.

When considering people resources outside your organization, find an agent who has not just expertise but status. Providing the help of a person with both special resources and unique status can send a double message: I value you; I want to help you grow. It also can be a special treat for the agent you select.

I had the opportunity to serve as the agent for a great mentor. I was hired by a large Northeastern bank to develop a two-day training program that would be taught to supervisors at various sites by a group of carefully selected managers. The program was designed and field tested and a series of train-the-trainer sessions was conducted. Linda Burgess was the senior project leader; Phil was one of the handpicked managers chosen to teach this new course. I got to know Phil very well during his week in training.

One day Linda called to hire me for a day. "I need your help," she began. "Phil has a particularly difficult group next month on the other side of the state, and I think he'd feel a lot more confident if you could be there the first day — sort of as his assistant."

Phil did great! He really didn't need my help. But I could see his relief when I arrived unexpectedly that morning an hour before his first participant appeared. And I learned a lot watching him find his own style in the new program.

Create a Self-Directed Learning Plan

"The most powerful contribution teachers can make to students," human resource development guru Leonard Nadler has said, "is to help learners become their own teachers." However, the gift of self-directed learning to the protégé can pose a threat to the mentor for whom letting go means feeling left out, unneeded, and undervalued. It takes great courage, compassion, and caring to let the bluebird teach itself to fly. Because it is counterintuitive to you as a caring mentor, you need to take steps to ease the transition.

Meet with your far-away protégé and establish a learning plan. (The sidebar at the end of this chapter shows the key elements in a strong plan.) Check the protégé's progress at longer and longer intervals — once a month, then once every two months, then quarterly, and so forth. The goal is to wean yourself out of the process, not just the protégé. Make sure the strategies for learning use resources available to the protégé. Protégés who take responsibility for their own learning will show greater motivation. The old saw, 'If the student hasn't learned, the teacher hasn't taught,' does not apply to adults. (It doesn't apply to children either, but that's another story.)

Learning cannot always be tied to a full-time, full-access relationship. Today's work world is far from stable, regular, or planned, but learning must continue if organizations are to adapt and compete. Tomorrow's master mentors will be enablers, not experts; supporters, not smart persons. They will search beyond the old horizons to provide resources for protégés in Guam, Paris, and San Juan — as well as Galveston, Peoria, and Building Four.

MENTORING WITH THE HELP OF TECHNOLOGY

My wife has a new car with both GPI and voice recognition technology. Hands free, she can control the radio, CD player, car phone, and climate control simply with voice commands. The GPI system literally talks her home if she is lost in an unfamiliar section of Dallas. "When do you think this car will be able to talk me through changing a tire or changing the clock when we 'fall back?'" she asked one day. The question started me thinking about the future mentoring capacity of artificial intelligence.

> "The only people who achieve much are those who want knowledge so badly that they seek it while the conditions are still unfavorable. Favorable conditions never come."
>
> — C. S. Lewis

Several years ago researchers announced the effective results of computers doing low-level psychotherapy. Simply by 'listening' to the response of the patient and providing targeted follow-up questions, the computer could lead the patient to helpful levels of self-awareness and therapeutic insight. While inappropriate for the treatment of many psychological maladies, it demonstrated that artificial intelligence technology could play a role in the helping professions.

We are moving fast on the frontier of artificial intelligence. Already in manufacturing facilities robotics are not only doing sophisticated assembly, but are teaching their human associates what they require in terms of maintenance and support. The medical field uses robotics for certain surgical procedures. Add the advances in voice recognition and you have the stage set for artificial intelligence mentors.

How can technology be best mined as a mentoring resource? While many of the possibilities are breathtaking, it is important to remember that computers are linear and rational, not intuitive and abstract. If the support needed is creative in nature, artificial intelligence may disappoint you. A computer can soundly beat you at chess, but is not likely to help you solve your challenges with self-confidence. Artificial intelligence can retrieve minute details for your benefit, but will probably not be able to make subtle connections between two seemingly unrelated pieces of information.

Mentoring with technology requires respect and patience. There is no such thing as a 'dumb computer.' The wisdom to be gained from any technological resource comes from the genius of its creator (a.k.a. programmer). And the maxim 'garbage in, garbage out' applies to the computer user too. Speak clearly and avoid jargon or colloquialisms. 'Easy as pie' might get you into a discussion about baking. 'Chilling out' could provoke a sudden drop in room temperature.

Mentoring with technology also requires continual updating and quality control. As humans we are constantly learning. Artificial intelligence is generally not a self-generating device and, without enhancements and continuous retrofitting, it can become obsolete very quickly giving you dated advice or misleading suggestions.

Mentoring does not always happen in the secure routine of a stable work site. With the business environment becoming more chaotic, more globalized, and more dependent on technology, wise mentors learn to coach on the run, at a distance, using all the technology available to them. Granted, the pace of a protégé's learning may be different from the pace of work, but the realities of speed and the uncertainties of permanent white water still color the learning experience. Protégés should not be denied the help of their mentor just because they are physically inaccessible. Wise mentors adjust to the realities of place. Wise mentors adjust to the realities of technology.

Elements of a Learning Plan

1. **My learning goal is:**
   (e.g., I would like to develop an effective customer-service survey for the customers in my area of responsibility.)

2. **Resources I will likely require:**
   (e.g., I will need to talk with the general manager at the site, review the marketing research section at the library, call the customer service departments of three well-known marketing research consulting firms, etc.)

3. **People I know who can assist me:**
   (e.g., I need to talk with our organization's marketing research director.)

4. **Barriers I am likely to encounter and how I might overcome them:**
   (e.g., I have an outage report due that I need to delegate to Sam; the two-hour catering meeting needs to be shortened to one hour and everyone notified; etc.)

5. **Timetable I expect to use in achieving my objective:**

6. **Checkoffs with my manager:**
   (dates and times)

7. **Other relevant notes on my learning plan:** ■

ACKNOWLEDGMENTS

No one writes a book alone. Many people gather around the solo author to transform rough words on a computer screen into polished prose on a printed page. This is my opportunity to thank the many who gathered with me. The task is a bit daunting, not unlike all those Academy Award winners whom we annually watch struggle under spotlight and camera to remember all the people to thank.

There were four teams who worked on *Managers As Mentors.* The Texas editorial team was headed by Leslie Stephen in Austin. Leslie demonstrated late-at-night, around-the-clock commitment to this book from the very get-go. She delivered her extraordinary management talents and creative strengths in a fashion that usually felt effortless and always seemed limitless. Jeff Morris helped her with the editorial 'heavy lifting' on the first edition, and Deborah Costenbader worked on both. This is the seventh book I have done with Leslie — enough said!

Randy Martin headed up the multi-talented, multi-tasking Ohio production team. Randy's dust jacket and creative text design combined into an overall look that exactly conveys the spirit of mentoring partnership. Randy and his Cleveland-based team also handled all the nitty-gritty details of turning several hundred thousand bits and bytes of electronic files into books on bookstore shelves — on time, with minimum author worry.

The California publishing team was led by Steve Piersanti, president of Berrett-Koehler Publishers. I know of no one who demonstrates more integrity, professionalism, and deep dedication to a true publisher-author partnership. His entire company delivers beyond-the-call-of-duty commitment. They all live their values. This is my fourth book (counting the first edition) with Berrett-Koehler and my fifth with Steve.

The Minnesota and Florida cheerleading team included my Performance Research Associates partners: Ron Zemke and Tom Connellan, both authors of several best-selling books. Each offered helpful suggestions, unique and partially baked ideas, and never-ending encouragement. Additionally, I received great feedback from reviewers Pat Stocker, Jeff Kulick, Sharon Wingron, and Sandra Chase. Finally, this book would not have happened without the emotional sustenance and ingenious inspiration of Nancy Rainey Bell. The subtitle of this book is really about Nancy. She is the best there is at building partnerships for learning. Our thirty-five-plus–year partnership, filled with mutual mentoring, has been a joyful crucible for learning. By her unconditional love, vast intellect, and unselfish devotion, she has taught me more about partnership than any person on the planet!

To all of you: Thanks.

NOTES

Page

[16]   **Peter Vaill's term 'permanent white water':** Vaill, *Managing As a Performing Art.*

       A 2000 McKinsey & Co. study: Fishman, p. 104. *Mentoring is now seen as one way:* "Emerging Work Force Study," p. 104.

[29]   **Extensive research shows:** Material on focus, feeling, family, and freedom adapted from *Instructing for Results*, by Fredric Margolis and Chip R. Bell, and inspired by Malcolm Knowles's *The Adult Learner: A Neglected Species.*

[42-47]   The Mentor Scale adapted by permission of the publisher from *At Your Service*, by Chip R. Bell and Ron Zemke. Copyright © 1995, Quality Resources, Inc. All rights reserved.

[45]   The FIRO-B® instrument is distributed by Consulting Psychologists Press, 3803 East Bayshore Road, Palo Alto, California 94303, (415) 969-8901. An updated version renamed Element B: Behavior is available from Will Schutz Associates, Inc., P.O. Box 1339, Mill Valley, California 94942-1339, (800) 462-5874.

[48]   Dialogue from the movie *The Empire Strikes Back*, George Lucas, Producer, Lucas Films Limited Production, 20th Century Fox release.

[52]   **"Or it has that talent....":** Sellers, "What Exactly Is Charisma?" p. 74.

       In her article: Oliver, "Mockingbirds," p. 80.

[111]   **"Shared vision is vital....":** Senge, *Fifth Discipline*, p. 206.

[127]   **"There is an energy field between humans. . . .":** May, *Love and Will*, p. 312.

[128]   **"[Deming] loved Japan. . . .":** O'Toole, *Leading Change*, p. 197

[129]   **"Until one is committed, . . .":** Murray, *Scottish Himalayan Expedition*, p. 206.

[134]   **"When we see that to learn. . . .":** Senge, *Fifth Discipline*, p. 279.

[141]   Lyric from "It's Alright, Ma (I'm Only Bleeding)." Copyright 1965 by Warner Bros. Music, renewed 1993 by Special Rider Music. All rights reserved. International copyright secured. Reprinted by permission.

[141-142] Questions adapted from Gary Heil, Tom Parker, and Rick Tate, *Leadership and the Customer Revolution: The Messy, Unpredictable and Inexplicably Human Challenge of Making the Rhetoric of Change a Reality*, pp. 59–60. Reprinted with permission.

REFERENCES

Barton, Kathleen. *Connecting with Success.* Palo Alto, CA: Davies-Black Publishing, 2001.

Bell, Chip R. *Customer Love: Attracting and Keeping Customers for Life.* Provo, Utah: Executive Excellence, 2000.

Bell, Chip R. *Customers As Partners: Building Relationships That Last.* San Francisco: Berrett-Koehler, 1994.

Bell, Chip R., and Oren Harari. *Beep Beep! Competing in the Age of the Road Runner.* New York: Warner Books, 2000.

Bell, Chip R., and Heather Shea. *Dance Lessons: Six Steps to Great Partnerships in Business and Life.* San Francisco: Berrett-Koehler, 1998.

Bell, Chip R., and Ron Zemke. *Managing Knock Your Socks Off Service.* New York: AMACOM, 1992.

Bell, Chip R., and others. *The Trainer's Professional Development Handbook.* San Francisco: Jossey-Bass, 1987.

Cohen, Norman H., *The Mentee's Guide to Mentoring.* Amherst, MA: Human Resource Development Press, 1999.

Connellan, Thomas K. *How to Grow People into Self-Starters.* Ann Arbor: The Achievement Institute, 1991.

Castaneda, Carlos. *The Teachings of Don Juan: A Yaqui Way of Knowledge.* Berkeley, Calif.: University of California Press, 1968.

Dass, Baba Ram (Richard Alpert). *Be Here Now.* San Cristobal, New Mex.: Lama Foundation, 1971.

Dass, Baba Ram (Richard Alpert). *The Only Dance There Is.* Garden City, N.Y.: Anchor Press, 1974.

DeGeus, Arie. *The Living Company: Habits for Survival in a Turbulent Business Environment.* Boston: Havard Business School Press, 1997.

DePree, Max. *Leadership Jazz.* New York: Doubleday, 1992.

Edvinsson, Leif, and Michael S. Malone. *Intellectual Capital: Realizing Your Company's True Value by Finding Its Hidden Roots.* New York: HarperBusiness, 1997.

"Emerging Work Force Study." *Business Week*, March 1, 1999.

Fishman, Charles. "The War for Talent." *Fast Company*, August 1998.

Goldsmith, Marshall, Beverly Kaye, and Ken Shelton, eds. *Learning Journeys.* Palo Alto, Calif.: Davies-Black Publishers, 2000.

Goldsmith, Marshall, Laurence Lyons, and Alyssa Freas. *Coaching for Leadership: How the World's Greatest Coaches Help Leaders Learn.* San Francisco: Jossey-Bass, 2000.

Greenleaf, Robert K. Servant Leadership: *A Journey into the Nature of Legitimate Power and Greatness.* New York: Paulist Press, 1977.

Harvey, Jerry B. *The Abilene Paradox and Other Meditations on Management.* New York: Lexington Books, 1988.

Heil, Gary, Tom Parker, and Rick Tate. *Leadership and the Customer Revolution: The Messy, Unpredictable and Inexplicably Human Challenge of Making the Rhetoric of Change a Reality.* New York: Van Nostrand Reinhold, 1994.

Howard, Pierce J. *The Owner's Manual for the Brain: Everyday Applications from Mind-Brain Research.* Austin: Leornian Press, 1994.

Jourard, Sidney. *The Transparent Self: Self-Disclosure and Well-Being.* New York: Van Nostrand Reinhold, 1971.

Kiser, A. Glenn. *Masterful Facilitation: Becoming a Catalyst for Meaningful Change.* New York: AMACOM Books, 1998.

Knowles, Malcolm. *The Adult Learner: A Neglected Species.* 4th ed. Houston: Gulf Publishing, 1990.

Kram, Kathy E. "Phases of the Mentor Relationship." *Academy of Management Journal* 26, no.4 (1983): 608–625.

Lane, Tom, and Alan Green. *The Way of Quality: Dialogues on Kaizen Thinking.* Austin: Dialogos Press, 1994.

Leonard-Barton, Dorothy. *Wellsprings of Knowledge: Building and Sustaining the Sources of Innovation.* Boston: Harvard Business School Press, 1995.

Luft, Joseph. *Group Processes: An Introduction to Group Dynamics.* 2nd ed. Palo Alto, Calif.: National Press Book, 1970.

Mackay, Harvey. *Swim with the Sharks without Being Eaten Alive: Outsell, Outmanage, Outmotivate, and Outnegotiate Your Competition.* New York: Morrow, 1988.

Margolis, Fredric, and Chip R. Bell. *Instructing for Results: Managing the Learning Process.* San Diego: Pfeiffer and Co., 1986.

Margolis, Fredric, and Chip R. Bell. *Understanding Training: Perspectives and Practices.* San Diego: Pfeiffer and Co., 1989.

May, Rollo. *Love and Will.* New York: Dell Publishing, 1969.

McClelland, David C., J. W. Atkinson, R. A. Clark, and E. L. Lowell. *The Achievement Motive.* New York: Appleton-Century-Crofts, 1953.

McClelland, David C., J. W. Atkinson, R. A. Clark, and E. L. Lowell. *The Achieving Society* Princeton, N.J.: Van Nostrand Company, 1961.

Murray, Margo. *Beyond the Myths and Magic of Mentoring.* San Francisco: Jossey-Bass, 1991.

Murray, W. H. *The Scottish Himalayan Expedition.* London: MacMillan and Sons, 1950.

Oliver, Mary. "Mockingbirds." *The Atlantic Monthly*, February 1994.

O'Toole, James. Leading Change: *Overcoming the Ideology of Comfort and the Tyranny of Custom.* San Francisco: Jossey-Bass, 1995.

Pirsig, Robert M. *Zen and the Art of Motorcycle Maintenance: An Inquiry into Values.* New York: Doubleday, 1976.

Powell, John. *Why Am I Afraid to Tell You Who I Am?* Rev. ed. Allen, Tex.: Tabor, 1990.

Putman, Tony, Chip Bell, and John Van Zwieten. "Artificial Intelligence and HRD: A Paradigm Shift." *Training and Development Journal,* August 1987.

Rogers, Carl. *On Becoming a Person.* Boston: Houghton Mifflin, 1972.

Saint-Exupéry, Antoine. *The Little Prince.* New York: Harcourt, Brace and World, 1943.

Sellers, Patricia. "What Exactly Is Charisma?" *Fortune,* January 1996.

Senge, Peter. *The Fifth Discipline: The Art and Practice of the Learning Organization.* New York: Doubleday, 1990.

Shea, Gordon F. *Mentoring: How to Develop Successfuy Mentor Behaviors,* Menlo Park, CA: Crisp Publications, 1992.

Vaill, Peter B. *Managing As a Performing Art: New Ideas for a World of Chaotic Change.* San Francisco: Jossey-Bass, 1989.

Vaill, Peter B. *Spirited Leading and Learning: Process Wisdom for a New Age.* San Francisco: Jossey-Bass, 1998.

Zachary, Lois J. *The Mentor's Guide: Facilitating Effective Learning Relationships.* San Francisco: Jossey-Bass Inc. 2000.

Zemke, Ron, and Chip R. Bell, *Knock Your Socks Off Service Recovery.* New York: AMACOM, 2000.

Zemke, Ron, Claire Raines, and Bob Filipczak, *Generations at Work,* New York: , AMACOM, 2000.

ABOUT THE AUTHOR

Chip R. Bell is a senior partner with Performance Research Associates, Inc., and manages its Dallas office. PRA consults with organizations on ways they can build long-term customer loyalty. He has served as consultant or speaker to such major organizations as IBM, GE, AAA, Microsoft, State Farm, Motorola, Marriott, Lockheed-Martin, Ritz-Carlton Hotels, 3M, Pfizer, Eli Lilly, USAA, Royal Bank, GlaxoSmithKline, Merrill Lynch, Verizon, Chevron, Sears, Harley-Davidson, and Victoria's Secret. Additionally, he has served as a visiting instructor at Cornell University, Manchester University (UK), and Penn State University. Before starting a consulting firm in the late 1970s, he was vice president and director of management and organization development for NCNB Corporation (now Bank of America). He was an infantry-unit commander with the elite 82nd Airborne Division in Vietnam and in 1970 served on the staff of the Instructional Methods Division of the U.S. Army Infantry School.

Chip is the author of fourteen books including *Customer Love: Attracting and Keeping Customers for Life, Customers As Partners, Managing Knock Your Socks Off Service* (with Ron Zemke), *Knock Your Socks Off Service Recovery* (with Ron Zemke), *Beep Beep: Competing in the Age of the Road Runner* (with Oren Harari), *Dance Lessons: Six Steps to Great Partnerships in Business and Life* (with Heather Shea), *Instructing for Results* (with Fredric Margolis), *Understanding Training* (with Fredric Margolis), *The Trainer's Professional Development Handbook* (with Ray Bard, Leslie Stephen, and Linda Webster), and *Clients and Consultants* (with Leonard Nadler). He has also contributed chapters to *The Sales Training Handbook, The Training and Development Handbook, The Handbook of Human Resource Development, Coaching for Leadership, Learning Journeys,* and *The Best Practices in Customer Service.*

His articles on training and learning have appeared in such professional journals as *Training and Development* (now *T+D*), *Training, HR Magazine, Personnel Journal, Workforce Training News, The Toastmaster, Educational Leadership, Adult Training, Adult Leadership, Storyteller's Journal, Journal of European Training* (UK), and *Journal of Management Development* (UK). Chip's articles on leadership and mentoring have appeared in *Management Review, Biz, En-*

trepreneur, Quality, Supervisory Management, Journal of Quality and Partici-
pation, Advanced Management Journal, Executive Excellence, Executive Directions,
The Journal of Management Consulting, Services, Quality Digest, Staff Digest and
Today's Leaders.

Chip R. Bell
Performance Research Associates, Inc.
25 Highland Park #100
Dallas, Texas 75205-2785
Phone: (214) 522-5777
Fax: (214) 691-7591
E-Mail: chip@chipbell.com
Websites: www.chipbell.com,
            www.socksoff.com
            www.beepbeep.com

INDEX

ABOUT THE TYPE
Text and headlines are set in Kennedy Book GD
from Galapagos Design Group.
Call outs are in Equinox ICG
from Image Club Graphics.